Teaching for Thinking

*A Program for School Improvement
Through Teaching Critical Thinking Across
the Curriculum*

ᴄ⁊

Teaching for Thinking

A Program for School Improvement
Through Teaching Critical Thinking Across
the Curriculum

ℰↄ

JOSEPH P. HESTER

Carolina Academic Press
Durham, North Carolina
1994

Copyright © 1994, Joseph Hester

Library of Congress Card Catalog Number: 93-73552
International Standard Book Number: 0-89089-563-5
Printed and bound in the United States of America.

Carolina Academic Press
700 Kent Street
Durham, NC 27701
(919) 489-7486 FAX (919) 493-5668

Contents

❧

Preface

⁊

The public pressure on schools to demonstrate their worth is acute. This pressure has encouraged educators to focus on relatively narrow but tangible goals, e.g. those associated with competency-based education or standardized achievement test scores. This understandable response overlooks a fundamental fact: the quality of learning is determined by the quality of the processes used in learning. Too often we act as if quality if found only within the goals we pursue (measurable test results), while the methods we use in reaching these goals are qualitatively neutral. Educators have argued that the norms for evaluating the quality of education are discovered within the context of learning, namely, within the processes, strategies, and methods used by teachers.

Teaching-for-thinking is an important educative process. Thinking, critically and creatively, is also an important feature of productive societies, and a characteristic of successful schools. As such, teaching-for-thinking commits us to respect the intelligence of teachers and students. This is a practical lesson, but one that is difficult to learn. Instructional improvement with an emphasis on intellectual processes is and should continue to be teacher-dependent and student-focused.

Research demonstrates that learning can be improved and that scores on standardized achievement tests can be raised if thinking skills (and skill combinations) are infused into teaching on a regular basis. Teaching Critical Thinking Skills is a program committed to school improvement through teaching and learning improvement. It is inconceivable that schools can improve without improvement in teaching and learning. Educators need to ask themselves what they would have 21st Century men and women to be. Teaching-for-thinking emphasizes creating individuals who are capable of doing new things, not simply of repeating what others have done. Teaching-for-thinking aims to develop individuals who are creative and inventive; who are able to verify information for themselves and not simply accept everything they are offered.

We now know that when we emphasize thinking, the outcomes of learning are improved. Teaching-for-thinking is not, therefore, just another educational fad. Rather, it is a comprehensive plan for improving the process of schooling. Educational improvement will include all subject and skill areas, and to be complete, it will also include the improvement of the mental capabilities of teachers and students. When teachers begin to develop their own thinking and problem solving skills, they will more likely try new ideas in the classroom. Also, when teachers are learning and are given the freedom to be innovative, the curriculum becomes teacher-proof and the rewards of teaching, intrinsic. Teachers with a vision to share usually speak that vision and act on it to create "learningful" classrooms. Teaching Critical Thinking Skills is committed to the restoration of educational vitality. We believe that vitality can be restored to our schools and the quality of teaching improved by strengthening the means used to achieve intellectual goals and objectives. This is our mission.

Introduction

❧

Like learning, thinking is incremental and developmental. This conclusion—based on knowledge of how students learn—implies that some intellectual processes are more basic than others and are required for mastering more complex thinking processes. For example, the skill of inference-making is necessary for problem solving, for decision-making, and for using the scientific method. Teachers should be sure they understand the thinking skill composition of major intellectual processes. Teachers should teach both the thinking skills as well as the problem solving processes normally used in learning activities. Chapter One organizes these thinking skills according to developmental level and under essential learning principles. The teacher will be able to utilize these skills in teaching activities leading to more complex thinking processes.

Children are normally holistic learners involving their minds and bodies in a dynamic kinesthetic relationship. They move back and forth from whole to part and from part to whole when learning about ideas, a new skill, or about people, places, events, and things. Science educators are today reminding us that older students need to place their hands as well as their "minds" on science and math activities. This, they tell us, will involve the total child in the processes needed to improve cognitive skills. Kinesthetic learning and the back-and-forth movement from whole to part and from part to whole take on a recognizable form as children enter school and engage in "systems" learning (the learning of subjects through pre-established norms, written, oral, and audio materials). Our role as teachers is to tap into their seemingly natural learning modalities, provide for them careful nurturing, and prepare them cognitively and emotionally to become life-long and independent learners.

Teaching Critical Thinking Skills is an endorsement of thinking as the most fundamental process leading to school improvement. We believe that the empowerment of the intellect will enable both teachers and students to create their own futures and work positively toward fulfilling their lives. By strengthening the intellect, teachers and students will be able to influence change and cope with diversity in more creative ways. Thinking, both creative and critical, is the energy that drives history. Thinking creates knowledge, understanding, meaning, and provides for us a frame of reference through which we view the world. Thinking is also analytic, providing the ability to solve problems and evaluate competing alternatives. The development of thinking ability, as a major focus for our schools, will revolutionize education, teaching, learning, our values and society.

The material in Teaching Critical Thinking Skills is divided into three sections: (1) Setting a Foundation For Thinking; (2) Rebuilding For Critical Thinking; and (3) Organizing For Critical Thinking.

Setting A Foundation begins with an explanation and justification of "The Effective Thinking Skills Model" (ETSM). This model is research-based and easy to use. The teacher's mental abilities, dispositions, and understanding of "thinking" are prerequisite to the application of creative and critical thinking skills in the classroom. The Effective Thinking Skills Model is conceptually based, defining the essential areas (principles and skills) of thinking. It then orders them across developmental levels and blends them with effective teaching strategies. ETSM is designed for teacher use and provides both the theoretical and practical knowledge needed for infusing thinking skills into daily lesson plans.

Chapter Two reminds teachers that there are critical flaws in untrained thinking. Thus, to be effective, we need to consciously and consistently seek new ways to improve the quality of our own thinking. The means by which we are able to change from a dominant reliance on didactic teaching to teaching-for-thinking is called "cognitive restructuring" (CR). CR implies that teachers will deliberately learn how to modify their teaching for thinking skills improvement; acquire the skills of critical intelligence for themselves; model these behaviors within the teaching/learning environment; and provide creative and critical thinking opportunities in daily lesson plan activities. Teaching-for-thinking is both a conscious and deliberate behavior.

Rebuilding teaching to include teaching-for-thinking is an essential

---

Four Steps Leading to Cognitive Restructuring

L—Learn how to teach for thinking
A—Acquire thinking skills for yourself
M—Model thinking within the classroom setting
P—Provide opportunities for students to think

---

part of school improvement. School improvement specialists have given us a vision of what our schools can become. They have led school-improvement teams through year-long improvement activities. Now is the time to focus on the quality of teaching and the development of effective instructional practices. These will include the defining of learning objectives, remodeling teaching strategies, and bringing feedback correctives to bear on the remediation of academic deficiencies and enrichment practices to bear on those skills and knowledges which have been mastered (see pages 00–00). A significant number of studies have found that increased academic achievement can be accomplished by raising expectations for all students. Also, a number of critical studies have shown that the infusion of critical thinking into teaching practices every day enhances student performance in all areas of the curriculum.

Because schooling is about thinking, we find it imperative that all phases of teaching include the development of the creative and critical intelligence of all students. The goal of teaching-for-thinking is the ability to understand one's environment in such a way as not to be totally controlled by it, but to be able to impact upon it with innovation, invention, and discovery. We desire students to become independent thinkers, creative problem solvers, and effective decision-makers. We also hope they develop a moral presence and a sense of fair-mindedness so their behaviors are not only characterized by intellectual prowess but also by living a life that can be interpreted ethically.

The improvement of thinking will include the improvement of learning in all areas of the curriculum. Thinking strategies should therefore be connected with those teaching strategies already proven effective for school improvement. Thinking skills improvement will occur best when thinking skill innovations are adjusted to and blended with existing teaching methods, particular school organizational patterns, and the dispositions of individual teachers. Teaching Critical Thinking Skills will assist teachers with this process.

Organizing a school or school district for teaching-for-thinking is perhaps one of the most important steps for successfully infusing thinking skills into the school curriculum. Research and innovation come to nothing if not applied in useful and meaningful ways. Section Three offers some practical suggestions for utilizing The Effective Thinking Skills Model by restructuring teaching strategies, training teachers, and monitoring the program's development and outcomes. We have learned through experience that teachers and administrators usually get around to asking the question "How might we...?" Anticipating this question, Chapter Eight offers a plan for organizing a school/school district for teaching-for-thinking. This plan is an organizational outline which each school and school district will be able to refine and develop for themselves.

As we begin this process, we should avoid false expectations. A plan can become effective if diligently developed and consistently followed by those committed to its implementation. Change will not come overnight nor will it ever be complete—but we are expected to change. We can understand the problem of educational improvement, work to modify our own thinking and the thinking of our students, and sell our vision of what education can become to others with whom we work. A thinking school is a learning school. This we all know and understand. Learning will improve as teachers focus their attention on thinking, become good thinkers themselves and teach for thinking at all times. This is our task and our responsibility.

PART ONE
Foundation for Thinking

The purpose of *Teaching for Thinking* is quite clear: it is the task of wisely mastering those thinking processes which are characteristic of the intellectual mind. To become aware of our motives for teaching, motives that may conflict with the function of preparing students intellectually for the Twenty-First Century, is to begin to grow beyond them under the guidance of awareness. To become aware of motives that accord with mental growth is to grow in them.

We begin with becoming aware of who we are and why we are. Self-identification and recognizing essential educational purposes are the foundational stones upon which we can begin to rebuild our teaching practices. There is a distinction to be made between process and revision. We need to keep in perspective the personal, social and educational forces that influence teaching. Teaching-for-thinking should become a systematic quest to reconstruct our basic assumptions and the practices that flow from them. Purposeful reconstruction will be more and more in evidence as teachers learn the power-function of human reasoning processes.

Two areas need our attention as we begin the process of creating a foundation for teaching-for-thinking. First, we must understand the conceptual base for thinking and organize this base in such a way as to improve teaching and learning. Second, we must then come to an under-standing of ourselves—how we think and how we can restructure our own thinking processes. Upon this foundation—one which is conceptual and the other which is pragmatic—we will be able to begin the process of rebuilding our own teaching practices to include thinking skills and reasoning processes.

Education that emphasizes the intellect is an invitation to learn—to think, in the largest possible perspective, about the weightier, more stubborn problems of human life. It is an invitation to wonder, to question, speculate, reason, and fantasize—to join the eternal a search for wisdom. Education for thinking not only provides instruction in thinking skills and related cognitive processes, but it also allows students to think. Conceived of in this way, education is a do-it-yourself enterprise. Thinking is a skill. Skills require practice and application. Thinking is something one learns to do.

> *Not the Power Man, not the Profit Man, not the Mechanical Man, but the Whole Man, Man in Person, so to say, must be the central actor in the new drama of civilization. . . . If technics are not to play a wholly destructive part in the future of Western Civilization we must now ask ourselves, for the first time, what sort of society and what kind of man are we seeking to produce?*
> — Lewis Mumford, *In the Name of Sanity (1954)*

CHAPTER ONE

Creating a Conceptual Base for Thinking

ए3

BACKGROUND

Since the early 1980s, the school improvement process has generated one innovation after another. Today, many of those innovations have lost their impetus and new ones have risen to take their place. Those which remain have demonstrated tangible results in student learning, teacher effectiveness and school leadership. The integration of these strategies into a workable program for school success has already begun (Guskey 1990). One clear task remains: *the integration of strategies-for-improvement with an effective thinking skills program.* This thinking skills program must also be supported by current research and developmentally ordered across the whole school curriculum. The thinking skills defined by this program should then be integrated with those school improvement processes that have effectively improved student learning and achievement. Careful planning will ensure that skillful thinking will be infused within the context of curriculum and instruction.

In this chapter we propose to:

1. show the need for the infusion of critical thinking skills into the school curriculum;
2. present a practical model for including critical thinking in the practice of teaching; and
3. explicate this model by demonstrating its applicability and consistency with current cognitive and developmental research.

PRINCIPLES OF "LEARNINGFUL" ORGANIZATIONS

Peter M. Senge (1990) says, "...forget your tired old ideas about leadership. The most successful corporation of the 1990s will be something called a learning organization....As the world becomes more complex and dynamic, work must become more 'learningful.' " What is true in business is also true for our schools. Schools, to become truly successful in educating our youth, must also become "learningful" institutions. They must discover how to tap both teachers' and students' commitment and capacity to learn at all levels and in many different ways.

Senge presents the following processes as building blocks for a vision-led and "learningful" organization. We believe these can be adapted to schools.

Systems Thinking. Systems thinking is a conceptual framework, a body of knowledge and tools that has been developed over time to make the purposes and methods used in teaching clearer and to help us see how to change them more effectively. Systems thinking does not mean ignoring complexity. Rather, it means organizing complexity into a coherent story that illuminates the causes of problems and how they can be remedied in lasting ways.

Personal Mastery. Mastery means more than dominance. It also means a special kind of proficiency. A master craftsman does not dominate pottery or weaving. The educators within our schools who demonstrate a high level of proficiency are able to consistently realize the results that matter most deeply to them. They are able to do this by becoming committed to their own lifelong learning and to that of their students.

Measures of educational effectiveness, such as the SAT, reveal that we are fast becoming a nation of illiterates and semi-illiterates. In 1990, verbal scores on the SAT fell to their lowest point in a decade and still trail quantitative measures of academic performance. Personal mastery, on the other hand, is the discipline discovered in those who are continually clarifying and deepening their personal vision, focusing their energies, developing patience, and pursuing knowledge and understanding. Our schools' commitments to and capacities for learning can be no greater than those of their students, teachers, and administrators.

Mental Models. Senge defines "mental models" as *deeply ingrained assumptions, generalizations, or even pictures or images that influence how we understand the world and how we take action.* Mental models are the frames of reference or windows through which we view the world around us. They include our personal biases as well as those opinions based on reason and objectivity. They are the familial and cultural assumptions/presuppositions that define our philosophies and give us direction and motivation. They also include our feelings and beliefs about special people or events in our world.

To teach-for-thinking may mean changing who we are or what we have become. Thus, we start by turning the mirror inward and learning to unearth our own internal pictures of the world. Our personal assumptions about teaching need to be brought to the surface and held rigorously to scrutiny. Do we have the courage to carry on "learningful" conversations with our colleagues and the public whom we serve, conversations that balance inquiry with advocacy where we expose our own thinking effectively and make it open to the influence of others?

Building A Shared Vision. Teachers are the frontline leaders in education. If any one idea about leadership has inspired people from the earliest times, it is the capacity to hold a shared picture of the future they seek to create. No school (or any organization for that matter) has sustained a measure of greatness and longevity without goals, values and missions that become deeply shared by its teachers. Teachers are the ones who provide images of the future for our youngsters, as well as the motivation to use individual strengths to pursue their dreams and bring to fruition their loftiest aspirations.

A common identity and sense of destiny do not imply "sameness." Rather, they imply the existence of a genuine vision where students and teachers excel and learn, not because they are told to do so, but because they want to. A personal vision is worthless to a school or a school district unless it becomes a shared vision. This will involve conversations in which shared pictures of the future are unearthed that foster genuine commitment and enrollment rather than compliance. A leader cannot dictate a vision, no matter how committed.

Team Learning. "Learningful" organizations share the discipline of team learning. Team learning begins with dialogue, the capacity of team members to suspend judgment and enter into genuine "thinking together." To the Greeks *dia-logos* meant a free-flowing of meaning through a group, allowing the group to discover insights not attainable individually. Senge reminds us that the discipline of team learning also involves learning *how to recognize the patterns of interaction in teams that undermine learning.* Team learning is vital because teams and not individuals are the fundamental learning unit in modern society. Unless teams can learn and avoid defensiveness, the organization cannot learn.

We are suggesting that schools should become "learningful" organizations. This we understand will involve the way teachers, administrators, students and parents perceive themselves and their world, and define their roles with respect to the goals of learning. At the core of a "learningful" school will be a shift of mind—from seeing oneself as separated from others to connected with others in the system of learning by internal and social purposes, from seeing the problems of school improvement as caused by someone or something "out there" to seeing how we frequently create the problems that we experience. A "learningful" school is a place of revitalization, where teachers and students are able to come together and find meaning in their intermingling experiences, experiences which are at once creative and self-generative.

Real learning gets to the heart of what it means to be human, for through learning we recreate ourselves over and over again. The phrase "you're never too old to learn" should therefore be understood positively and not negatively. Learning is a reaffirmation of the quality and growth throughout the life span. It is no accident that in some schools students learn poorly and that teachers do not think or are not allowed to think. Where there is no teaching-for-thinking, we find people who are incredibly proficient at keeping themselves from learning. This phenomenon is correctly called "skilled incompetence" (Argyris 1990). In these schools there is also an absence of systems thinking, personal mastery, the creation of new mental models and the examination of old ones, a shared vision, and team learning.

The active force in any school is its teachers. School improvement can only be brought about through teachers who are able to think and learn. Experience has taught us that most teachers have their own way of thinking and teaching. If they are not sufficiently motivated to rethink and redevelop their own styles of teaching, there simply will be no growth, no gain, and no progress. School improvement specialists understand the necessity of tapping the potential of teachers. They also realize that to ensure lasting effects, school improvement must become more than hype—mottos, logos and inspirational speeches. To teach-for-thinking requires teachers who are committed and willing to redefine their understandings and practices. They will be asked to give up a reliance on didactic instruction, workbooks, ditto masters and the verbal giving of "knowledge." Instead, they will be asked to focus on infusing thinking skills into each lesson, to coach for thinking skills improvement, and to provide discussion opportunities, exploration of knowledge areas, and research/writing opportunities. To teach-for-thinking implies the creation of "learningful" environments—the establishment of the conditions that enable students to lead the most enriching lives they can. The idea of *life long learning* implies personal growth and the spirit of the "learningful" school. This spirit rekindles in us the spirit of enlightenment which is able to affect change and bring about a renewal of our schooling efforts. Senge reminds us that"...personal mastery goes beyond competence and skills....It means approaching one's life as a creative work, living life from a creative as opposed to reactive viewpoint."

Visions can be exhilarating. They are able to create the spark, the excitement, that lifts a school out of the mundane and into the spirit of challenge and renewal. In a school, a shared vision changes people's relationships with each other and with the system of schooling itself. A shared vision initiates trust and a common identity. Can we share the vision of a "thinking" school? Can we come together with a shared sense of purpose and operating educational values that provide renewal and revitalization to our schools? We cannot have a "learningful" school without a shared vision, a common purpose, and an agreed upon plan for reaching our goals. Without *a pull toward a goal* which teachers truly want to achieve, the forces in support of the status quo can be overwhelming. Vision establishes an overarching purpose. Our vision is of a school that teaches-for-thinking, shares this vision within itself and to the community at large, and fosters risk-taking and experimentation.

SCHOOL IMPROVEMENT THROUGH THINKING

To ensure that students learn to the optimum of their ability, we must teach them to think critically and creatively. They should also learn to utilize formal reasoning processes (the scientific method, research methods, logical reasoning, etc.) to increase their learning productivity (Marzano et al. 1986). In a poll of professional educators, in the early 1980s nine out of ten respondents said that better instruction in thinking skills should be a major priority in educational planning for the coming years (ASCD 1983). Government and business leaders and a sizeable segment of the American public support this same initiative (National Commission 1983).

Beginning in this century, schools in the United States have considered mastery of thinking or reasoning a major goal of public education (Dewey 1910). There is evidence to suggest that we still have a long way to go in achieving this goal (Report 1981; Walton and Toch 1982). As early as 1960, E. Paul Torrance (1963) warned,

> tomorrow's schools will place an emphasis not only on learning but on "thinking." More and more insistently, today's schools and colleges are being used to produce men and women who can think, who can make new scientific discoveries, who can find more adequate solutions to impelling world problems.

Torrance's tomorrow is today's reality. However, looking back to 1960, we discover that although thinking has been researched and recommended, the application of these findings in textbooks, college teacher courses and classroom strategies is sadly lacking. On a large scale, the call for teaching-for-thinking has not been heard.

For example, Torrance (1990) has assisted Ginn and Company since 1966 with the development of a creative thinking strand in the Reading 360 and Reading 720 programs. He says, "Since it required new skills, it created problems for both the field consultants and most teachers; the creativity strand was largely unused." Torrance indicates that he was discouraged by Ginn's failure to train their field consultants in creativity and the use of creativity materials and by their decision to drop the creativity strand. The 1990 publication of Torrance's *Incubation Model of Teaching* represents his extension of the word "thinking" to include creative thinking skills along with rational/critical thinking skills.

During the past decade we have witnessed a steady decline in SAT scores, especially the verbal portions. We are fast becoming a nation of non-readers and some predict that we are heading toward a situation where the bulk of our society will be word-illiterate. We have also seen a thirty-year neglect of an embarrassing dropout rate, the growth of negative and unproductive values, a sagging economy, and the rise of violence in our schools. Together, these indicators should initiate a new urgency about teaching-for-thinking. In January, 1990, our political leaders gave us a vision of a country composed of skilled and literate workers and citizens. But skilled, literate workers in today's biotechnical society must not only be capable of performing basic reading, writing and mathematical operations; they must also be capable of sustained, systematic and accurate thought.

We perhaps owe this idea to John Dewey (1916) who wrote, "Mind is not a name for something complete in itself; it is a name for a course of action in so far as it is intelligently directed; in so far, that is to say, as aims, ends, enter into it, with selection of means to further the attainment of ends."

In this same spirit, Rene Dubos (1962) remarked, "The persons most likely to become creative and to act as leaders are not those who enter life with the largest amount of detailed, specialized information, but rather those who have enough theoretical knowledge, critical judgment, and discipline of learning to adapt rapidly to the new situations and problems which constantly arise in the modern world."

Critical and creative thinking, when infused into every lesson in every classroom, will enhance student performance in all areas of the curriculum including the ability to analyze issues and form judgments, find solutions and evaluate conclusions, to research and negotiate, as well as anticipate the actions of others (Arredondo and Block, 1990). Critical thinking requires respect for using intelligence to make decisions.

In his extensive work on critical thinking, Barry Beyer (1987, 1988) provides the following steps to thinking skill improvement and believes that these tasks can be accomplished by teachers who wish to improve the learning of thinking skills among their students:

1. Identify and clearly define a core of thinking skills that ought to be taught.
2. Identify as precisely as possible the components of each of these skills.
3. Provide direct, systematic classroom instruction in how to use these skills in all appropriate content areas and across all appropriate grade levels.

4. Devise and implement developmental curricula that integrates the teaching of selected skills within various content areas.

5. Devise measures of competence in the use of thinking skills that are congruent with the skills that we have chosen to teach and that are as valid and reliable as possible.

THINKING AS PROBLEM SOLVING

The *Effective Thinking Skills Model* follows these directives and is built from a conceptual base which defines "thinking" as "problem solving." Cognitive scientists (Hunt 1982; Newell and Simon 1972; Johnson-Laird 1983) define "thinking" as essentially a problem solving process. We have learned that a person is confronted with a problem when he wants to make sense out of some experience, a bit of new information, or when he wants something and does not know immediately how to get it. All thinking is, therefore, an effort to arrive at some desired goal; hence, thinking is problem solving. Johnson-Laird observes, "...thinking is not a thing, but a process....a continual movement back and forth from thought to word and from word to thought. Every thought tends to connect something with something else, to establish a relationship between things. Every thought moves, grows, and develops, fulfills a function, solves a problem."

We therefore begin our discussion of "thinking" by considering humans as problem solvers. When this hypothesis is made, we are able to examine the steps leading to problem resolution and discover clues about the nature of human thinking, thinking skills and reasoning processes. This examination will guide our efforts and help us make provisions for teaching-for-thinking. Viewing thinking as essentially a process of problem solving enables us to generate four fundamental thinking processes characteristic of all learning operations:

1. **Perception and recognition**. A person perceives the raw data of experience and processes these perceptions, recognizing the patterns generated by memory, which allow the components of the problem to emerge. This knowledge forms the conceptual base for meaning and understanding.

2. **Organization**. In Johnson-Laird's view, every thought tends to-

connect something with something else, establishing a relationship between things. Hence, to think organizationally implies
the development of the skills of classification, seriation and sequencing.

3. **Storage, retrieval, and transformation of data**. Experience provides the information from which common sense is generated.
These mental models (perceptions and organizations of data)
not only initiate the transformation of the incoming data into
meaningful inputs but ignite memory, imagination and reason
to transform the new data into useful information (understandings).

4. **Reasoning**. In the course of carrying out problem solving activities, one will notice whether any step or series of steps decreases
the distance to the goal of problem resolution. If this occurs, the
person will continue with it; but if not, the person will move on
to other steps. If the entire program fails to carry one to the desired goal, the person can either quit, modify the process, or
change the problem itself. This requires a high level of reasoning
ability, including the skills of inductive and deductive inference,
quantitative and qualitative analysis, and the ability to work in
problem solving teams.

A Special Note

Paul Torrance (1979) reminds us:

*Recent theories of creativity in psychiatry and psychology in the United
States and other Western countries also support a concept of creativity as a
higher mental process. Earlier explanations of creative thinking by psychia-
trists and psychologists treated creativity as a regressive thought process, lower
than rational, logical thought processes...*

*Rollo May has maintained that creative processes are not irrational but
are "suprarational," bringing the intellectual, volitional, and emotional
functions into play all together. He believes that creative thinking represents
the highest degree of emotional health and is the expression of normal people
in the process of actualizing themselves. He sees it as a process involving a re-
alistic encounter with a problem, intense absorption and involvement,
heightened consciousness or awareness, and interrelating.*

Figure 1.1: Summary Chart
Thinking as Problem Solving

Thinking is the process of connecting bits and pieces of experience with other bits and pieces of experience to establish a relationship between things, to move from the simple to the complex or break the complex into component parts for study and understanding. This process grows and develops, fulfills a function, and solves a problem. The goal is understanding through explanation. Understanding depends on knowledge and experience.

1. **Facilitating skills** based on perception and recognition. These skills include observation for comparison and identification of similarities and differences found in spatial relationships, linking and matching perceptions and memories, and the organizational skills of classification, seriation and sequencing.

2. **Processing skills** based on classifying the environment in which one lives. These skills include explaining, interpreting, evaluating, drawing conclusions, formulating and testing simple hypothesis, as well as oral and written communication. These skills are needed for the mental representations of one's environment, the interpretation of goals in relation to it, and the kinds of actions a person must perform to attain these goals.

3. **Operational skills** based on the storage, retrieval and transformation of data. The transformation of information into useful forms for solution finding and decision making includes the skills of inductive reasoning, quantitative interpretation, deductive reasoning, social judgement, group interaction and communication. Herein lies the essence of the problem solving process.

4. **Basic argument forms.** When the thinking skills and problem solving processes have been learned, they can then be transformed into formal reasoning procedures—inductive, deductive, analogical and evaluative reasoning—that are able to give precision and consistency to one's thinking.

5. **Creativity skills.** Creativity skills are based on the idea that thinking, to be effective, should be open-ended, flexible, innovative and fluid. Osborn (1963) and Torrance (1990) provide insights into the nature of creative thinking and models for creative learning which enhance critical thinking by allowing for more insightful and risk-taking responses.

THE EFFECTIVE THINKING SKILLS MODEL

Both theory and practice indicate that an effective synthesis of class-room teaching research and thinking skills research will produce better learning outcomes and respond to a growing pressure to serve all students (Marzano et al. 1990). *ETSM* represents a blending of research on thinking skills, effective schools, mastery teaching and learning, creativity, teaching/learning styles, cooperative learning, and developmental theory. From effective schools research (Arrendondo & Block, 1990 and Guskey, 1990) we can generate the following guidelines for improving teaching and learning:

1. Innovative strategies should share common goals and common premises.
2. No single innovative strategy can do everything.
3. Innovative strategies should complement each other.
4. Innovative strategies need to be adapted to classroom conditions.
5. Finally, when a well-conceived combination of innovative strategies is used, the results are likely to be greater than those attained by using any single strategy.

These components provide the skeletal framework for building a

Figure 1.2: The Effective Thinking Skills Model *(ETSM)*

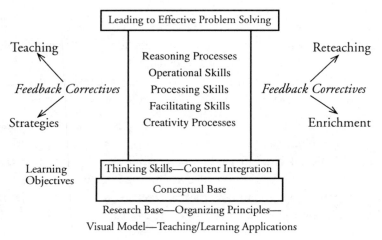

thinking skills model that works. *ETSM* has one basic goal: **to provide improved learning outcomes.** The aforementioned components can be applied at any grade level and within any content area. The key to their effectivenss is "...adjusting to the innovation and adjusting it to fit the conditions of particular classrooms " (Guskey, 1990).

Learning Objectives

The learning objectives of *ETSM* bring thinking skills and reasoning processes to bear on content and related learning skills. Important to the application of thinking skills in any subject area is that they be developmentally appropriate for the group being taught and relevant to learning the content lesson, concepts and content-associated skills. Teaching-for-thinking will have little impact on student learning if a consistent and relevant application of appropriate thinking skills and reasoning processes is absent. Marzano (1988) has provided a framework through which teachers are able to adapt teaching-for-thinking to classroom practices. This framework is one of the structural models for *ETSM*.

Effective schools and mastery teaching research support the development of clearly defined learning goals and objectives. The model developed in *The Philosophy For Young Thinkers* series (Hester & Vincent 1983–1990) divides learning objectives along a continuum from the concrete to the abstract processes and dimensions of teaching/learning. These objectives include the following basic knowledge categories:

1. Facts "that which is...,"
2. Concepts "mental/abstract categories of facts,"
3. Values "beliefs and assumptions (mental models) brought into the classroom by teachers and students,"
4. Skills "learning and thinking skills used to master both factual and conceptual information and evaluate strongly held values."

Teaching which exposes children to concepts, as well as thinking skills and skill combinations, helps them develop their appropriate cognitive capacities. Factual content cannot be considered an end unto itself. Rather, facts are the "stuff" (knowledge, information, ideas, events, etc.) used to support, explain, and clarify important cultural concepts. Beliefs and assumptions (values) should also be examined, both historically and personally. Teaching for understanding requires that the full complement of facts, concepts, values, and skills be brought to bear on the learning process in developmentally appropriate ways.

Following is a lesson plan guide which utilizes these four categories of thought. This lesson plan guide can be extremely helpful for infusing thinking skills and conceptual analysis into regular lesson materials. This guide also serves as a useful reminder to include objectives, strategies and feedback correctives into every lesson, every day.

A Reminder...

The classroom is the ideal place to provide the experiences that students need to develop formal thinking skills and concepts. Without planned experiences and developmentally based instructions, students do not appear to develop formal reasoning on their own.
                                                        —Patricia Arlin, 1987

Instructional Practices

It is simple: teachers must be inspired to teach and students to learn. Looking back over my own twenty-five years in college and public school classrooms, motivation seems to be the key ingredient. Although most teachers are under intense pressure to follow prescribed instructional procedures, teaching style, motivation and innovation require teachers to seek out the best means available to them to affect positive learning outcomes. Frank Smith (1986) reminds us that "our schools should not remain places where the enormous potential of the human brain is systematically eroded, and possibly destroyed. The invasion of education by instructional programmers must be turned back now." For every teacher there seems to be a seemingly natural teaching style. Students also have unique learning styles. One fact remains clear to us: all students—young and old—are naturally capable of learning. It will be sensitive and imaginative teachers who inspire students to learn, who stimulate their interests and challenge their intellectual abilities.

Instructional practices proven effective for the improvement of learn-

Figure 1.3: Lesson Plan Guide

1. Learning Objectives
Subject area:
Lesson title:
Major Facts:

Skill focus:
        Subject related skills:
        Thinking/creativity skills:
        Major lesson concepts:

Resources:
        Text:
        Curriculum Guide:
        Other:

Student objectives:
        The student will...

2. Instructional Practices
Strategy Choices:
        Mastery teaching/learning
        Teaching/Learning Styles
        Creativity (creative problem solving)
        Paideia approach
        Whole Language/integrated learning
        Thinking Skill Infusion

Teaching Procedures:
        The Teacher will...

3. Feedback Correctives
Evaluating (on-going assessment and testing)
        For mastery:
Summative:
Re-teaching: (to those who have not mastered lesson:)
Enrichment: (for those who have mastered lesson)

        Choices for re-teaching and enrichment include:
            Cooperative learning
            Mastery learning
            Learning styles
            Paideia coaching/seminar
            Metacognitive discussions

ing include the following:

Mastery teaching/learning. Both of these programs share a common assumption that virtually all students, regardless of their backgrounds, are capable of learning just as well as our best students do. Presseisen (1987) and Sternberg (1984) support this hypothesis and remind us that any student's intelligence can be trained. Mastery learning utilizing frequent assessment and feedback correctives (Block 1989; Bloom 1968; Guskey 1985; Spady 1988) and mastery teaching (Hunter 1979, 1982) have been shown to be effective in the improvement of learning outcomes.

Developmental approaches. The literature of school improvement has not fully addressed the issue of providing skills, materials, methods and activities that are *developmentally appropriate*. Yet, the results of Piagetian "type" programs (Piaget 1971, 1974; Langford 1989; Lowery 1989) indicate that any strategy—to be successful in the improvement of student learning—must be consistent with the social and cognitive levels of students (Thornburg 1988). By attending to research from the developmental data base, educators will be able to establish instructional practices which students are able to comprehend, appreciate and functionally employ while learning.

Teaching and learning styles. The information now available on teaching and learning styles (Butler 1986; Gregoric 1979, 1982; Keirsey and Bates 1984; Herrmann 1989; and Torrance 1979; 1990) is extremely helpful when teachers are planning alternative instructional approaches, especially for corrective and/or enrichment (lesson extension) activities. More effective student learning outcomes become possible when attention is given to teaching modality and learning disposition.

Creativity. Creativity theory is consistent with and supportive of thinking skill development. Creativity can be thought of as a skill of thinking when the dispositional modalities of originality, flexibility, risk-taking and incubation are applied to reflective processes and thinking skills. The body of creativity research now available to us has virtually been ignored by states in the development of teaching procedures and measures to evaluate teaching. Also, textbook companies have ignored creativity (Torrance 1990) because of the difficulty of measuring creative behaviors and identifying the variables associated with creative learning.

Creativity can add depth and dimension to learning which cannot be adequately measured in quantifiable tests. Creativity can also assist with the improvement of teaching and learning. Creativity research reminds us to view students as centers of learning, pass on the responsibility of learning to students, and empower students with the skill and motivation to become independent and lifelong learners.

Feedback correctives and enrichment. Essential to learning are feedback correctives based on continual, consistent assessment and summative evaluations. Where correctives are not needed, enrichment can be provided to extend and reinforce learning. Coorperative learning (Johnson and Johnson 1987; Slavin 1983), mastery learning, and learning styles research provide a theoretical basis for remediation and lesson extension through enrichment activities. Cooperative learning ("mind builders") was used extensively in *Cartoons For Thinking* (Hester, Killian and Marlette 1984; 1987) to extend and enrich the concepts and skills focused upon in each lesson. The above mentioned teaching techniques are especially valuable when planning alternative instructional approaches which are designed to strengthen and deepen a student's cognitive abilities.

Thinking Skills: Principles and Applications

The purpose of the *Effective Thinking Skills Model (ETSM)* is to provide teachers a means for using innovative instructional practices with critical and creative thinking skills and skill combinations (Guskey 1985; 1986; 1988; 1990). These include the following:

1 Developing a conceptual base that carefully defines "thinking" and provides a delineation of thinking skills across the curriculum;

2. Stating learning objectives that integrate thinking skills with whatever subject is being taught by specifying content objectives, content processes, related concepts and values, and supportive thinking skills;

3. Organizing a developmentally appropriate sequence of thinking skills supported by thinking skills research and carefully linked to learning improvement;

4. Outlining major instructional practices that have been proven effective, providing opportunity for teacher selection;
5. Utilizing assessment techniques for developing correctives and enrichment opportunities to improve learning capability;
6. Developing a problem solving framework fully usable in the classroom and supported by the development of thinking skill processes.

As this model *(ETSM)* unfolds, it is important to interconnect its various components and blend teaching strategies to reinforce and strengthen the consistency and effectiveness of teaching/learning. According to Guskey, a careful blending of these components will enable teachers to promote the synthesis of innovative instructional practices: "...achieving optimal integration of innovation will not be easy, but doing so is essential if school improvement efforts are to sustain their momentum, continue to expand, and bring about the kind of results for which the innovations were intended."

When these strategies are applied consistently, some fairly persuasive evidence exists to document improvements among less able learners, average learners, and more able learners (Nickerson et al. 1985). Others (Bloom 1988; Soled 1986; and Mevarech 1989) have discovered that when teachers focus on higher mental processes within the mastery learning format, both the thinking and the knowledge levels of students improve.

An essential key to increased learning improvement is the interlacing of appropriate thinking operations with complex content knowledge in a manner which enhances meaningful thought (Bransford et al. 1988). We are indeed excited about the prospect of being able to bring thinking skills to impact on the learning of facts, concepts, and values, and of being able to integrate the essential components of school improvement into instructional practices that have already proven effective for student learning.

Creating a Skills Base for Thinking

Interacting with children and youth has taught us and others (Clark

1979), that the experiences of childhood are forces which mold and develop their cognitive abilities. These experiences remain with children throughout their lives and are especially important as a source of cognitive strength and emotional stability. By the time a youngster enters school the groundwork for educational success (or failure) has been laid. The school-age child is already in a natural cycle of cognitive development that may or may not be retarded by environmental conditions. The teacher's responsibility is to intercept the child in midstream of socio-cognitive development as quickly and efficiently as possible. The teacher is required to quickly learn the child's storehouse of concept-memories and experiences, and then discover the breadth of the child's reasoning abilities. Within this framework of experience and ability must be created learning activities that extend the child's interest and excitement about learning. There can be no substitute for the expertise harvested by experience nor the knowledge that students are able to reveal about their own abilities and cognitive readiness.

An important feature of *ETSM* is the developmental ordering of thinking skills and the refinement of the micro-cognitive processes necessary for teaching and learning. The teacher's task is **not** that of pushing students vertically from one developmental stage to another. Rather, it is to reconsider the broad range of ability-potential through which the student is now passing, to reinforce, extend and modify these skill patterns through the integration of process with content and the utilization of feedback correctives which allow skills coaching, remediation, and enrichment.

The skills definitive of thinking as problem solving can be divided developmentally, supported by cognitive science research, organized and broken into mico-skills appropriate for learning and instruction (see "Summary Chart: Thinking as Problem Solving" in this chapter). *ESTM* roughly divides these skills into three groups for instructional purposes: facilitating skills (spanning the Piagetian levels of pre-operations and early concrete thinking), processing skills (the movement of early concrete and high concrete into transitional thinking), and operational skills (the movement of transitional to early formal and high formal thinking). These levels are defined in the following manner:

Facilitating skills, grades K–3 are those micro-thinking processes necessary for performing all other thinking operations. They are requisite for mastering basic subject-related skills (number operations, reading, writing, and research/comprehension skills). The research base for this skill stage is provided by Piaget (1926), Piaget and Inhelder (1969), Lowery (1989), Sternberg (1979), Inhelder and Piaget (1964), Langford (1989), and Whiteley (1985).

This stage is characterized by perception and organization abilities, skills necessary for inferential thinking, predicting, and problem solving operations. Learning at this stage should include as many hands on activities as possible and be discovery-based. Younger children are primarily sensory learners and their organized perceptions become a part of their conceptual make up. The basic organizational functions at this stage are classification (the grouping of information according to established patterns), seriation (the ability to place items in order gathered from experience), and sequencing (the ability to construct an ordered progression of objects and/or events).

Processing skills, grades 4–6 build on facilitating skills. At this stage students are able to process ideas simultaneously and group them according to multiple attributes (subordinate/superordinate relationships). Students are now able to conserve quantity, length and number while grouping and are able to process multiple properties and concepts at the same time.

As students move into higher concrete operations they develop reversibility skills and are able to undo operations mentally, permitting the thoughtful exploration of various procedures with the ability to return to the beginning wherever and whenever necessary. Students can now use words and symbols to stand for concrete objects, thus lifting them from the limitations of concrete operations and facilitating the transition to early formal thought.

Processing skills lend themselves to teaching by inquiry and lead students into more formal reasoning as they learn to utilize skill combinations in goal-oriented learning activities. It is now that the curriculum should become more conceptually and process-based with factual content called upon to explain, enrich, and clarify the understanding of concepts. Inquiry includes the following micro skills: explaining, using multiple descriptors, cause/effect understanding and usage, hypothesis formation, interpreting and drawing conclusions, evaluating and classifying relationships, utilizing analogy and metaphor, and creating two-and three-dimensional models.

Although inquiry processes resemble problem solving and include many of the same procedures as early formal reasoning, there is a fundamental difference—problem solving and formal reasoning require the ability to reason abstractly, utilize propositional thinking (see chapter six), and make logical deductions. On the other hand, inquiry is tied to concrete thinking, factual information and the use of sensory (discovery) learning. Inquiry is therefore less formal, less structured and partakes of hands-on learning in which fully developed scientific reasoning is not required.

At the high end of concrete thinking, inquiry includes concept analysis, simple inferences, evaluation using multiple descriptors, inductive processes, and the ability to understand simple analogies and metaphors. One purpose of inquiry is to allow the student to mature in his or her thinking ability. As the student matures, s/he will make a gradual transition from high concrete to early formal thinking. This transition will be discussed fully in chapter six as a stage normally characteristic of middle school youngsters.

Operational skills, grades 7–12 are characterized by the ability of students to think abstractly and propositionally. This includes the ability to use formal reasoning and formal problem solving procedures, including quantitative and qualitative analysis. The student is now learning to use thoughts, ideas and concepts that have no readily apparent tangible or concrete referents. Thought is now brought to bear on multiple possibilities in order to explore the manifold hypotheses that lie before them.

A characteristic of this stage is combinatorial reasoning. Students can now organize, reorganize and apply purpose to process and product. As they move from high concrete through the transition to early formal thinking, students should be encouraged to become more flexible in their judgments and tolerant of ambiguities, keeping in mind that solutions, facts, values and methods of knowing change from generation to generation and, perhaps, from culture to culture.

As solution-alternatives present themselves, students are now able to evaluate alternatives using traditionally established criteria. They are beginning the move into formal thinking and create their own criteria for making judgments. Although students at this stage are able to think abstractly and logically, these skills do not occur naturally and, during the transitional phase, will occur inconsistently (Arlin 1987). According to Piaget (1978), skills must be taught, practiced, refined and reinforced at each stage of cognitive development if they are to become a part of the students' repertoire of thinking abilities. Patricia Arlin comments:

> Without planned experiences and developmentally based instruction, students do not appear to develop formal reasoning on their own. This should not be surprising since Inhelder and Piaget seemed to imply this in their definition of the eight formal schemata as " ...concepts which the subject potentially can organize from the beginning of the formal level when faced with certain kinds of data, but which are not manifest outside these conditions."

On the following pages the *Effective Thinking Skills Model* is presented in detail covering

facilitating skills: perceptual and organizing principles focusing on generating and clarifying ideas;

processing skills: the analysis of patterns and relationships utilizing the principles of conservation and reversibility ; and

operational skills: abstract reasoning and propositional thinking leading to effective problem solving and decision making.

Following, in chapters four, five, and six, these skill areas are developed in detail with suggestions for teaching and thinking skill infusion.

Figure 1.4: The Effective Thinking Skills Model, K–3

Facilitating Skills	Based on perception/recognition of the concrete environment. Organizes experiences or objects in some reliable way.			
1. *Research Base*	Piaget	Preoperational (can symbolize) to early concrete		
	Lowery	Preschool level 2, Primary/upper elementary		
	Summary	Attention is given to properties of objects with one to one correspondence; multiple objects with one property; and two or more properties—beginning at about age eight.		
2. *Organizing Principles* Focus: Generating/Clarifying Ideas, Accurate Observation, Use of Evidence	Perceptual Skills	Sensory learning: patterns/relationships in relation to past experiences; exploring, manipulating, discovering, forming concepts		
	Organizing	The ability to classify, seriate, sequence the data of experience		
3. *Teaching Applications*	**K**	**1**	**2**	**3**
Skills of Perceiving	Observing, collecting, describing	Comparing, characterizing by resemblance	Exploring, finding new relationships	Looking for inter-relationships
Skills of Classifying	Listing, matching by known category	Sorting by similarities & differences	Concepts: belonging/not belonging	Multiple groupings by shared properties
Skills of Seriating	Ordering by size, shape & color	Ordering by volume, pitch & tempo	Ordering by increasing/decreasing sound, pitch shade, color	Ordering by cause/effect relations
Skills of Sequencing	Reproducing objects in a sequence by model or by memory	Sequencing by actions, words & writing	Understanding sequence of natural events, language, time & stories	Ordering by cause/effect events
4. *Creativity*	Discovery learning/hands-on/manipulatives/intuition			
5. *Formal Reasoning*	Facilitating skills are the building blocks to higher thought			

Figure 1.5: The Effective Thinking Skills Model, 4–6

Processing Skills	Based on classifying the environment, creating relationships among groups of objects, and building superordinate concept groupings.		
1. *Research Base*	Piaget	Early concrete to late concrete and early formal thinking	
	Lowery	Upper elementary (simultaneous ideas) and middle school (superordinate/subordinate ideas)	
	Summary	Mentally combines more than one idea at a time; coordinates two or more properties at a time; some abstract ability	
2. *Organizing Principles* Focus: Analysis of Patterns and Relationships, Reasonableness of Conclusions	Conservation Skills	Can conserve quantity, length, and number while regrouping, and process multiple properties at the same time	
	Reversibility Skills	Can undo operations mentally, permitting the mental exploration of problems and the ability to return to the beginning of the problem. Words/symbols now stand for concrete objects	
3. *Teaching Applications* (extensive use of inquiry method and concept analysis teaching)	**4**	**5**	**6**
	Explaining using multiple descriptors and cause/effect relationships	Comparing and contrasting two or more situations	Using analogy & metaphor in explanations and interpretations
	Formulating simple hypotheses using "if, then" format; checking reliability of basic information	Modifying simple hypotheses; identifying, classifying assumptions	Using established single criteria & multiple criteria to test hypotheses
	Differentiating relevant from irrelevant data	Making predictions; inferring conditions and consequences	Evaluating hypotheses using multiple criteria
	Finding conclusions; making inferences	Making/evaluating alternatives	Generalizing and transferring concepts
4. *Creativity*	Inquiry learning using rational and intuitional abilities		
5. *Formal Reasoning*	Concept analysis, simple inference-making, evaluative and explanatory reasoning.		

Figure 1.6: The Effective Thinking Skills Model, 7–12

Operational Skills	Based on transforming information in different ways for specific purposes, then organizing knowledge in logical patterns	
1. *Research Base*	Piaget	Late concrete; early formal to late formal operations (embodies middle level period of transition from concrete to formal thinking)
	Lowery	Junior High (intentionality); Secondary (logical relationships)
	Summary	Systematic thinking; inconsistent at first; ability to evaluate inferences for consistency and coherency; ability to deal flexibly with ideas
2. *Organizing Principles*	Abstract Reasoning	The ability to use thoughts and ideas that have no immediate concrete referent
	Propositional Thinking	Bringing judgement/evaluation/logic to bear on statements embodied in propositions that claim factual status
3. *Teaching Applications*	Students from grades 7–12 will be making the transition from high concrete to low formal and high formal thinking. Grades 7–9 will be a time of transitional thinking in which there will be an inconsistent use of abstract (formal) operations. The following descriptors characterize this stage:	
	High Concrete: A systematic approach to problems but gives no evidence of being able to form general rules or abstractions from problems.	
	Transitional: Inconsistent use of abstractions and inferences; complete cognitive conquest of high concrete operations with some use of formal thought	
	Low Formal: Capable of abstract thought and making inferences but requires opportunity to develop formal thinking skills	
	High Formal: Clear evidence of formal reasoning. Reinforcement of formal operations is appropriate.	
4. *Problem Solving*	The problem solving model will provide a method for infusing critical thinking skills into teaching.	

CHAPTER TWO

Cognitive Restructuring for Critical Thinking

ఴ

ENCAPSULATED THINKING

Our role is to make teaching and learning better. The purpose of cognitive restructuring for critical thinking is to redirect and rebuild the practice of teaching, the teacher's mental logic, and, ultimately, the way students are permitted to learn within the structures of organized schooling. Saying this does not imply that we have lost faith in teachers. On the contrary, we certainly believe that teachers are able and capable of performing the job of preparing youth for the Twenty-first Century. Frank Smith (1986) tells us he spent three years at Harvard University's Center for Cognitive Studies exploring the incredible intellectual achievements of all young children. He comments: "I discovered the brutally simple motivation behind the development and imposition of all systematic instructional programs and tests— a lack of trust that teachers can teach and that children can learn." Given the intense pressures under which today's teachers work, cognitive restructuring will enable them to use teaching-for-thinking to make learning more efficient.

Teaching thinking is student-centered and achievement-oriented. It is neither prescriptive nor programmatic. It does not come from predetermined goals and objectives but rather is student-focused, linking seemingly natural ways of learning with cognitive level and style. A careful examination of teaching reveals its two interdependent functions: one is individual and the other is social.

The *individual* function of teaching can best be understood from the point of view of cognitive science, the role of which is to explain the workings of the human brain. An understanding of our "mental" framework is essential for those who desire to improve their thinking and their teaching.

In his marvelous book, *The Creative Brain*, Ned Herrmann (1989) has developed a whole-brain model from which is organized a whole-brain teaching and learning model. In this model the learning process is divided into two categories: *structured* (left) and *unstructured* (right). The structured mode is subdivided into two areas: (A) the area of *hard processing* dealing with logical, rational, critical, quantitative issues and activities, and (B) the area of *procedural activities* involving planned, organized and sequential elements of the learning process. The right side of the brain is more unstructured and therefore non-linear and non-verbal, involving visual, conceptual and simultaneous processing as well as emotional, expressive and interpersonal activities. The right brain is open-minded, experimental and emotional. The left brain is factually based, structured and controlled.

From whole-brain research, we learn, among other things, the following concepts:

1. Each person has his or her own style of thinking and learning that is okay and important.
2. Other different styles of functioning in that same environment are also okay and important.
3. Through training and learning teachers can access and use mental modes not thought to be available to them.
4. Teachers can further expand their creative and critical options if they so choose.

A chief function of Herrmann's whole-brain model is to shed new light on the creative/critical problem-solving process expressed in terms of brain quadrants and based on scientific study and observation. This model is supportive of the *Effective Thinking Skills Model* and provides a means by which we are able to integrate creative and critical behaviors into options for learning and productivity. In the second part of this chapter, *The Nature of Intelligence*, we will return to Herrmann's model in our discussion of data-driven and goal-driven learning.

The *social* function of teaching requires the assistance of the social and human sciences which together provide facts, models and insights into the sociocultural systems of acquiring knowledge and values. In his insightful book, *The Encapsulated Man*, Joseph R. Royce (1964) outlines Man's **four approaches to reality**: thinking, feeling, sensing and believing. These four modes of knowing flow from the nature of man, itself a product of nature and the environment. The *thinking* approach-process is based on rationalism which interprets reality either logically or illogically (see Herrmann's model above). The *feeling* approach-process is based on intuitionism which interprets reality either insightfully or non-insightfully. The *sensing* approach-process is based on empiricism which sees reality as a perception or as a misperception. Finally, the *believing* approach-process is based on authoritarianism which approaches reality as an accepted ideology or rejected delusion.

Society and culture, in which we all are encapsulated, provide our knowledge approach-process, either singularly or in combination with one or more of the four approaches to reality mentioned above. Royce reminds us that we are all victims of tribal conditioning because "we are each encapsulated within our cultures, and from the time we were infants we have taken on a way of looking at things which was handed down to us. This includes ways of looking at reality!" The point is clear—each approach to reality and its corresponding theory of knowledge involves certain assumptions ("mental models") from which our view of the world has evolved.

The relationship of these two vital aspects of our thinking (the individual and the social) can either limit our vision and the way we think, or enhance our vision by freeing us from our sociocultural limitations. The essence of encapsulation is to offer one approach to reality as if it were the approach. To restructure our thinking and teaching is to break through the several cocoons within which we are inevitably encapsulated and broaden our "reality image."

> *Indeed, I do not forget that my voice is but one voice, my experience a mere drop in the sea, my knowledge no greater than the visual field in a microscope, my mind's eye a mirror that reflects a small corner of the world, and my ideas—a subjective confession.*
>
> —C. G. Jung

Knowledge translated as "thought" is a cultural product, ever changing and channeled through language and the dialogue of social communication. This is the foundation of our "reality image" and is the reason that we can no longer afford to define "literacy" as being able to read and write at a certain culturally acceptable level. Rather, literacy is now understood as the ability to read, write and *reason* about what we read and write. Literacy requires a combination of approach-processes and learning styles. It shares all four brain quadrants as defined by Herrmann. Because educators are committed to an obsolete conception of literacy, students are leaving our schools without cultural knowledge and understanding. Young people, to become productive citizens, must cultivate that function of the mind called "thinking."

Schools, as we are aware, divide knowledge into culturally important cubicles of thought called "subjects" or "courses of study." Here the drama of learning, knowing and valuing is played out through the sociocultural process of course definition, curriculum guides and textbook selection. But caught up in this growing bureaucracy of "learning" is the transmission of culturally significant values and skills and the motivation to learn. What we teach in the classroom, knowingly or not, acts as a catalyst for social change by letting loose forces that produce their own effects, and those effects can be neither prescribed, predetermined, predicted nor prevented. They will be whatever future man, thinking for him/herself, decides they will be, for "thinking" implies nothing foreseeable about the conclusions to which it may lead.

To help students think about their perceptions, insights and beliefs is an aim of education, but we seem to be unaware of this purpose. To teach and encourage students to think for themselves is to entertain the lively possibility that they may reject some of our cherished preconceptions in favor of their own variety of meaningful living. We cannot have it both ways—educate and at the same time keep the student from having ideas of his/her own. We no longer can conceive of cultural literacy as a mechanical function. We have learned and are still learning the lesson that the elaborate and technological civilization we must operate requires millions of people able to construct and follow discursive thought. Also, the American industrial complex reminds us that the basic skills of our entry-level workers are simply not good enough to give us the kind of work force we need to compete in a fiercely competitive global market. This is no less than a survival issue for America.

What thinking can do is help students make themselves into the kind of persons they want to be. Thinking can assist students maintain self respect by granting them the basic right of self-determination. To teach-for-thinking, schools must change. They must treat students, not as future citizens, but as present human beings, not as a means to social betterment, but as ends in themselves. Many of our school problems will solve themselves when we leave institutions and institutional meaning in the background and begin to address individuals.

To accomplish this feat, teachers too must become unencapsulated. This means that teachers will:

1. be relatively free of petty prejudices and view life objectively;
2. view students as citizens of the world with loyalties to humans as humans forming the highest pinnacle of commitment;
3. be free of discrimination and value the freedom of mind and body of all others;
4. approach reality from the point of view of all four epistemological routes. This would prevent encapsulation and open the mind to new and novel areas of knowledge.

The unencapsulated person would be particularly interested in what F. S. C. Northrop has called *epistemic correlations* (1947). An epistemic correlation is simply an agreement reached through two or more valid approaches to reality. The implication is that truth is best found by approaching problems from differing points of view. While it does not follow that the person who approaches reality with all his faculties will necessarily penetrate the reality barrier any better than the monorail reality seeker, it does mean that his/her multi-approach will give multi-rewards in terms of living out one's full potential. Further, this person's image of reality is less likely to be distorted. Because of one's great effort at synthesis we would expect such a person to be highly self-actualized, integrated and holistic (the Eastern sense of reaching for *satori*).

This union of opposites has been a theme played out in both Eastern and Western cultures, in philosophy, religion and psychology. The implication has been that such a merging of opposites represents a creative union, thereby releasing the single greatest potential for individual and social growth—creative expression. Teaching-for-thinking, both critical and creative, means more than restructuring lesson plans and introducing "thought" activities. It means changing who we are. The complexity of today's world demands a total approach and requires the type of openness that only the totally functioning or unencapsulated person can provide.

> *If the doors of perception were cleansed, everything would appear to man as it is, infinite. For man has closed himself up till he sees all things through the narrow chinks of his cavern.*
> —William Blake

Arthur W. Combs (1981) writes:

> The future demands effective problem solvers and citizens willing and able to deal effectively with themselves and each other in the solution of human problems. It requires open-system thinking and an emphasis on values, processes, human problems, and the human condition. Furthermore, an educational system that hopes to prepare youth adequately for the future must be concerned with student feelings, attitudes, beliefs, understandings, values— the things that make us human—as well as with student behavior.

John Dewey understood the impossibility of not teaching values. Cognitive restructuring for critical thinking will involve all cognitive processes, including what Kohlberg called "cognitive moral processes." Students are inevitably influenced by the school, its teachers, curriculum and structure. Teachers and other adults have their own ways of thinking, their own values-orientation. Students also have unique ways of thinking about life and values. As Kohlberg (1972) reminds us:

> Among other implications for the teacher, this notion suggests that if the child is a moral philosopher, then the teacher must be also.

The building of an unencapsulated atmosphere in the schoolroom does not happen by chance. It springs from the educational philosophy and moral commitments of the educator, his/her communicated belief that the school and the classroom has a human purpose. In short, promoting cognitive development requires a conviction on the part of the teacher to also become a better thinker. This implies a mental openness and flexibility in which the teacher listens carefully to the child's ideas and ways of thinking and honors these thoughts rather than seeking conformity between the student and the teacher. This last point is important. The philosopher E. A. Burtt (1965) insightfully explains to us that most of our perceptions, hence thoughts, fit into "the standard habits that perceivers in general, or perceivers in our cultural milieu, have formed." Burtt concludes that "finally, and most important, what is perceived is relative to the interests of the perceiver, which express varying degrees of emotional force." This is revealed in three distinguishable ways:

1. What is perceived is often perceived through some interest. Wishful perception occurs just as frequently as wishful thinking.
2. Even when no outright error occurs, we perceive objects, events, persons, etc. under the influence of a controlling interest which "colors" or biases what is perceived and what is thought.
3. The relationship perceived between object/situation and its environment constitute an interest-selection from various alternatives. According to Burtt, "*perception* then is no mere passive reception of what an object tells us, but an *interaction* between perceiver and object, in which each plays an essential part, and among the factors that play a crucial part on the side of the perceiver is his controlling interest."

Also, we reemphasize the point that, to a large degree, thinking is not only environmental, but developmental. Experienced and respected child development experts are warning us against two widely different educational concepts that may prove detrimental to the students' cognitive development. The first is the traditional "pressure cooker" theory that the best school is the one that teaches the most in the shortest time. Thus, the pressure is on to teach reading, writing and mathematics at an ever earlier age, often skipping phases of understanding in the process.

The second is the "permissiveness" theory usually associated with "free" schools and "open" classrooms. It rejects not only pressures but even discernible structures of teaching content. Children often move haphazardly from one activity to another, guided largely by what interests them at the moment. If middle school curricular builders are not careful, the "permissiveness" label will soon be applied to their efforts at constructing a middle level curriculum on the "needs," "interests," and "personal characteristics" of middle level learners without seriously taking into consideration the content curriculum handed down and changed by time through the Western cultural tradition (Beane 1990).

Jean Piaget (1974) has also spoken against the "American dilemma" of trying artificially to speed up a child's learning process. He reminds us that unless children are given a continuing chance to use and test their developing abilities, their intellectual growth will be stunted: "we need pupils who are active, who learn early to find out by themselves, partly by their own spontaneous activity and partly through materials we set up for them." The goal, of course, is to create men and women who are capable of doing new things. This is attained by a mixture of discovery and subtly controlled structure, leading students through the natural succession of their developmental phases.

Cognitive restructuring for critical thinking simply means we need to modify our teaching so that more children will learn to reason effectively about what they read, write, see and hear. We must provide students with the thinking skills that enable them to analyze, elaborate upon, and extend the ideas with which they are dealing. This is the conception of literacy that must take us into the Twenty-first Century. It is impossible to say how important or how difficult it will be for administrators to strive and hold out for curricula that afford time for this kind of truly literate learning.

Burtt reminds us:

> facts of observation do not always speak an unambiguous message with a clear voice. When they do so speak—when all thinkers agree on their occurrence and proper interpretation—one can appeal to them with confidence to settle any relevant question. And most facts in most situations do fill this role successfully. But there are times when inquirers are forced to realize that the questions: What is and

what is not a fact? Which facts are and which are not relevant to a given problem? are questions whose answers are not simple and obvious. The answer depends on the criteria taken for granted by whoever happens to be observing the facts involved.

THE NATURE OF INTELLIGENCE

Keeping in mind the nature of encapsulation, our first task is that of examining the nature of human intelligence. We should also remember that reliable cognitive mechanisms may be an antidote to error but are not a corrective to ignorance. Knowledge and insight are gained through a process of interaction which is constantly affected by emotion and cultural conditioning. Knowledge comes clothed in different social garments and cultural fabrics. E. A. Ellwood, in his *Methods of Sociology* (1933), reminds us that "it is only as we eliminate the personal equation that science becomes possible." But knowledge only comes through the personal sieve. Thus, can we ever gain reliable thinking? Is there any hope for cognitive objectivity? Or, can we only hope for a high truth ratio among the beliefs that our culture allows us to hold? We must openly grant that whatever is perceived and whatever is thought is seen and brought to cognition within the framework of personal interests. Spinoza discovered that through knowledge of our emotions, reason and feeling, we can win a stable union that was impossible to win before. Metacognitive activities used by teachers and students should not only examine the process of critical thinking but also discover the role of sociocultural and individual subjectivity within the thinking process.

To "win a stable union" is a hopeful promise. Without the promise and possibility of objectivity, we never could have embarked on such a precarious adventure as suggesting the restructuring of thought and the teaching-for-thinking. Critical and creative thinking may generate very few beliefs as they are caught up in conforming to and being restructured by cultural expectations. Thus, we stress mastering the skills commonly associated with critical and creative thinking. We also emphasize exposing our motives, attitudes and values that either permit or prevent us from revising our fundamental presuppositions. There is a distinction to be made between the process of revising as it takes place under the play of accidental forces and as it becomes a conscious and systematic quest for cognitive restructuring aimed at critical objectivity.

Motivation plays the dynamic role in the revision of thinking. This sociocultural, affective, persistent, nagging and risk-taking aspect of cognition is the source of intellectual power that demands to be perfected. Intellectual power allows us to use reliable cognitive mechanisms—critical analysis, problem-solving, creative thinking—to break the chains of ethnocentrism characterizing our encapsulation. Intellectual power also helps to establish a relatively large number of solution alternatives and brings them to bear on accepted belief and tradition. Torrance and Myers (1971) conclude that "...motivation is the key to learning."

Cognitive restructuring becomes more than acquiring a new set of "thinking" skills or revising an old set of mental operations. More than either of these, CR is the application of intelligent processes that are able to combat and relieve ignorance, not simply error. At any time and in any age we measure the power of intellectual leaders by their ability to question established beliefs and to open their minds to the possibility of novel solutions. The intelligent teacher is capable of relieving ignorance in students by:

1. extracting and examining the assumptions and unexamined beliefs of their culture, thereby generating new knowledge for conceptual and critical consideration;
2. understanding that knowledge and wisdom are always capable of being improved and that verified knowledge today may not be final tomorrow; and
3. being able to solve more problems by using these new processes and the information they generate in consistently reliable ways.

Thought of in this way, intelligence is the capacity to bring intellectual power and cognitive reliability to bear on significant human problems, to utilize inquiry successfully; to find answers and solve problems and to respond to the ever-changing universe which is uncovered using this knowledge to adjust, restructure and evaluate the goals we have set before ourselves.

The inquiring mind is guided by the assumption that anything and everything can be improved. Change, from this perspective, can be for the better. The task of the inquiring mind is to find out why this is true.

We are capable of continued cognitive growth, not only in the particulars of common sense and experience but in the underlying cognitive processes that transform our lives, and the former kind of growth requires the latter.

Conceived of in this manner, improvement in thinking comes to self-improvement. Our goal is to improve our knowledge and use of thinking skills and thinking processes, to become more open, free and mentally adventurous, and ready for innovation at every level. Daily alternatives present themselves either implicitly or explicity, and we choose to pursue some and not others of these waiting possibilities. Choosing which problems to solve and which ends to pursue is perhaps as important as the ability to use cognitive skills themselves. The process of sorting and assessing reflects our ability to think critically as well as our willingness to think at all. We cannot forget that motives, attitudes and beliefs are basic components of intellectual development.

But is it not quite fantastic to suppose that people can achieve such flexibility? Is not the power of tradition and habit, the need to feel secure in what we already believe, the longing to rest on authority so potent and pervasive that it would be out of place to expect in any but a few intellectual leaders an unreserved welcome to change? People (teachers) who are unaware of and unwilling to use their own mental power and who therefore need to depend on authority will continue to do so; they will ignore the disturbing pioneers and will turn to those whom they trust for guidance and emotional support.

Those who insist on living by error when truth has been glimpsed gradually pass from the scene. The future of our schools, of our country, lies with those who are not imprisoned by their present motives and presuppositions and *who can wisely reconstruct their way of thinking in detail and in whole.* Of course we all are committed to some presuppositions which we consider to be individually and socially important. But there are two ways of "committing oneself " to an ultimate presupposition— one is the way of making it an absolute dogma, and the other is the way of taking it as a relative guide, at present superior to any alternative but open to inspection and revision.

If we are always open to new insight, we can be quite happy when it proves, for a while at least, not to be needed. If we are not open, we will unhappily and anxiously resist when reality inexorably calls for change.

The one thing to avoid is an imprisoning attachment to any presupposition and the motive behind it, lest growth in wisdom and understanding come to an end. There is a need, from time to time, for each of us to break free of encapsulated assumptions and view the world from the point of view of "every" man. Wholeness and integration, both outwardly and inwardly, provide an optimal setting for the release of creativity, discovery, and innovation.'

WAYS OF KNOWING

Cognitive science provides two fundamental approaches to critical thinking: one that is **data-driven** and one that is **goal-driven**. Most individuals will use one of these approaches as their primary mode of problem solving. Cognitive restructuring for critical thinking calls for a careful synthesis of both of these approaches for more effective thinking and productive teaching.

These two differing modes of cognitive processing have been strongly emphasized by Neisser (1967) in his distinction between an early "pre-attentive" stage of thinking and a later "controllable," serial stage of thinking. Also, Lindsay and Norman (1977) make this distinction the cornerstone of their introductory psychology text and this idea surfaces again in the distinction Posner (1978) and Posner and Synder (1975) have made between *automatic* pathways activation and *conscious* attention. We discover this distinction being made once again by educational psychologists in their separation of right-brain cognitive processing and left-brain cognitive processing (Herrmann 1989). The left-brain is fact-based, structured and controlled. It is oriented verbally and processes information logically, rationally and quantitatively. This information is then organized, sequenced and controlled by a pre-determined procedure. On the other hand, the right-brain is open-ended, experimental and intuitive. It is oriented non-verbally and processes information visually, conceptually and simultaneously. This information is usually emotional, expressive and interpersonal.

The point made by Torrance (1977) and Herrmann (1989) is that effective critical and creative thinking requires the integration of both the

Data-Driven

The first approach to cognitive processing—that which is driven by data input—is relatively automatic, less capacity-limited, and more open to a variety of inputs and processes. It is also inductive because it is experience dependent. Learned early in life, data-driven thinking is more primitive, yet more flexible, than goal-driven thinking. We learn early by responding to stimuli and through trial and error. We learn to listen, perceive and adjust our thinking to the data that reality offers us. Every human act —walking, talking, perceiving, thinking—is a result of data-driven cognitive processing.

In the "Whole-Brain Teaching and Learning Model" developed by Ned Herrmann, the data-driven approach is located in quadrant "D." This area is what Herrmann calls "open minded" and is characterized by visual, conceptual and simultaneous cognitive processing. It is cerebrally linked to quadrant "A" which is factually based and experimentally linked to quadrant "C" which is based on feeling.

Goal-Driven

The second approach to thinking requires conscious control. Goal-driven thinking has severe capacity limitations, works in a serial capacity (one step at a time), and is usually begun as a response to internal signals. Because this approach is goal oriented, it is a consciously learned behavior. Thus, goal-driven behaviors are somewhat unnatural and focused on a particular problem. In the thinking classroom, goal-driven approaches come in such forms as the scientific method, creative problem-solving, research papers, and other direct skill-related assignments.

In Herrmann's model, the goal-driven approach is located in quadrant "B." This quadrant is characterized as being "controlled" and is defined as being organized, sequential and procedural. Quadrant "B" is structurally linked to quadrant "A" where both "A" and "B" are characterized as verbal. Quadrant "B" is limbically related to quadrant "C" and is cognitively contrary to quadrant "D."

right- and left-brain modes of information processing. Alone, either approach remains limited and ineffective. Herrmann says:

> The whole-brain model is dependent on all four quadrants being situationally available during all four phases of the creative process. Close one down and the creative potential is diminished. Close down two or more quadrants or phases and applied creativity as a desired outcome ceases. The process stops. Block the interactive path between the quadrants and the creative potential is again diminished because the basis of synergy has been denied.

During their earliest years, most people acquire a pre-attentive, data-driven and automatic mode of cognitive processing. On the playground and in the backyard, at home and in the school room—mainly through trial and error and a dependency on sensory perception—we acquired and became proficient at responding to our environment visually, simultaneously, conceptually (meaningfully) and with emotion. Because of early childhood experiences, which were less formal than school-oriented activities, this mode of thinking became more flexible, habitual and holistic, and less capacity-limited.

Being open-minded and experimental, this mode is more creative, more innately flexible, and allows us to handle many inputs from the environment at once. If we compare children at play with how they work in the school classroom, we can see the differences. On the playground they call to each other, swing, jump, run, play games and respond to each other. If we observe carefully, we will catch them doing many of these activities simultaneously. Children are naturally holistic learners and easily integrate their environments into manageable wholes.

But in traditional, desk-oriented classrooms, their holistic energy appears to fade and disappear. Mental wholeness and flexibility are forced into lockstep, serial and severely capacity-limited forms of learning. Within the classroom structure we discover goal-oriented learning and repetition. Children must sit in rows. Information now comes piecemeal from the teacher or through subject-area books. Also, the teacher has been trained to establish learning goals that give an overall focus to what is learned and, to a great extent, how it is learned. Evaluation, which is now quantitative and void of sociocultural meaning, is closely tied to both the procedural methods used in teaching and the lockstep curriculum guide. Never mind that these plans proceed along a linear line and fail to take into consideration how students learn, respond and process information.

The effort in America today to mass produce education has already yielded some negative results. Using the "assembly line" metaphor, the business and industrial communities are calling for the quality of educational production to increase, as if to say that teaching and learning are but a series of inputs and outputs. Those who control the economic purse strings of America have failed to find the quality for which they have paid and, like in their factories, have demanded teaching conformity and quality control through measurable evaluations of teaching and learning. Given the crisis in contemporary American schooling, this is not surprising. Only with a great deal of practice and under certain circumstances does the more controlled and less flexible mode of learning become automatic and productive. The effort to mass produce education from a common mold remains a cultural result of the industrial revolution, one whose day has certainly passed.

Recent research on problem solving (Larkin et al. 1980) has found that a move from goal-oriented to data-driven cognitive processing is associated with growing expertise. Hence, as teachers strive to improve their own thinking processes and apply these in the teaching/learning environment, they will actually be integrating the data- and goal-driven approaches to learning into their teaching. This integration will make allowances for student differences and learning styles. It will also provide a means through which they can learn naturally and in a holistic manner.

We have underscored the idea of developing intellectual capacity to both relieve ignorance and combat error. Thus, the purpose of cognitive restructuring for critical thinking is both social and intellectual. This purpose can be accomplished by (1) becoming more flexible in our own approach to problems that might run counter to accepted tradition; (2) utilizing data-driven thinking as much as possible; and (3) permitting these dispositions to govern our utilization of critical analysis and problem solving. The goal of cognitive restructuring is not only to restructure our methods for using critical thinking, but to redirect our teaching-for-thinking in order to fully integrate the data-driven and goal-driven modes of information processing that combine a natural and disciplined method approach to learning. In part two we shall return to this point by providing practical information about inquiry and problem solving as learning tools which provide for curricular integration and the pedagogical use of both goal-driven and data-driven thinking.

HOLISTIC THINKING

A basic assumption of general education is that the ability to reason lies at the heart of human intelligence. Humans have the capacity to improve the quality of living by using reason. Pragmatic reasoning includes making decisions concerning the improvement of the self through regulating one's diet, getting enough rest, selecting appropriate clothing and maintaining study habits. Of course, with more and more youngsters coming from homes that are only educationally or economically functional, pragmatic reasoning focuses more and more on survival than it does on the dominant values of our cultural traditions.

The essence of pragmatic reasoning is problem solving, the ability to solve immediate problems by producing alternative courses of action and selecting/applying one or more of these alternatives in daily living. The intellectual skills (critical thinking skills) that are the backbone of pragmatic reasoning are also used in combination with learning skills (reading, writing, adding, subtracting, analyzing, conceptualizing, etc.) to increase one's knowledge capacity and understanding of the human environment. Processes such as the *evaluation of assumptions*, the *analysis of arguments* for consistency and validity, the *assessment of evidence*, and the *evaluation of alternatives* are important thinking operations that provide an intellectual foundation for human living.

A problem remains that just might cause some difficulty in our teaching-for-thinking. We might find ourselves in a situation where we over-intellectualize thought processing and, in turn, over-organize our teaching-for-thinking. If we are not careful, we can over-analyze the processes associated with thinking and not allow enough time for students to apply thinking to the curriculum. While involved in the training of teachers and teaching children, we have sometimes wondered if "critical thought" is not a part of a past that is gone forever—a past that made the mistake of assuming that the world is rational and that humans can understand the world if only they develop their rational capacities. Today's emphasis on memorization, standardized tests and textbook subject learning is inconsistent with this rational hypothesis. Should we try to revive the past or leave it alone?

This is a cultural question, the answer to which defines our values and to a great extent, our perception of the purposes of education. Our belief in the power of thinking leads to the conclusion that if a problem cannot be settled by using critical and creative thought, then we are wise because we have at least identified a major problem in our social and educational organization.

Critical thinking and *creative thinking* are broad concepts. They include both rational and intuitive processes and utilize various capacities of the brain such as the power to rationalize and visualize. When we cut to the heart of critical and creative thinking, we discover that thinking is essentially a process of problem solving. In chapter one we outlined the micro-skills associated with problem solving. *ETSM* provides a developmental sequence of micro-thinking skills leading to more advanced problem solving and abstract reasoning procedures.

We can say that, fundamentally, problem solving is the application of intelligence to reality. As a technique, it cannot guarantee automatic success. There will always be a hiatus between aspiration and achievement. With finite ability and seemingly infinite problems, hope for future success seems to be diminished. When we survey the history of human achievement, we are given hope for the future, for there we learn that to possess a method is to have a way of deciding what questions may sensibly be raised and how to progress toward definite answers. Just surveying the rise of modern science, we begin to understand that this fruitful achievement could not have taken place without the visions of the two Bacons, of Bruno, of Galileo, and of Descartes—visions sufficiently articulated so that those who shared their hopes could observe the world around them in the **new framework** they provided and see something important that had not been clearly seen before.

Our present day educational responsibilities have changed little since the beginnings of the modern period of science, reasoning and questioning. Our responsibility is to assist students in becoming lifelong and independent learners. To help them "see" life and to "see" it whole means that we must provide for and facilitate their self-education, a privilege to take advantage of and not an exercise to be gone through blindly. In the last decade, we began to rediscover the missing element in public schooling—thinking. We now understand that ignorance means bondage—economic, political, social—and intellectual—whereas knowledge spells freedom. From the Eastern point of view, it is knowledge of one's self that brings true liberation. It is the bondage to one's inner drives and emotions that is the chief concern. While ignorant of them, one is inevitably their captive. As one becomes aware of their presence and nature, he/she no longer needs compulsively to express them in thought and action. The freedom from external constraint emphasized by the West can be sought under the guidance of reason, while freedom from inner bondage cannot be achieved by reason alone but needs to be transformed through a clearer awareness of their true place in our growing experience as a whole.

If we are not careful, we will once again lose the philosophic and historic sense of thinking. Today, thinking is being prepackaged and distributed in the educational marketplace in many different forms, some of which are not developmentally appropriate for certain ages and others of which provide an inconsistent and incomplete view of thinking itself. The teacher should thoroughly read the research on teaching-for-thinking before making programmatic and lesson plan decisions. Understanding the developments within this broad field is essential and focus is required for the application of appropriate skills within the teaching/learning environment.

The purpose of this book is to bring some needed organization and sensibility to the new emphasis on thinking in the public school classroom. In chapter one we organized the micro-skills of thinking developmentally and added to these skills those thinking processes (inquiry and problem solving) which form the core of more mature thinking operations. Because our students will continue to grow intellectually through their lifespans, it is necessary for us to provide for them a strong and sufficient foundation in thinking skill development. The challenges of the future will not wait for the intellectually unprepared nor the mentally timid. The future requires mentally flexible and critical thinkers. Students at every age should be educated in the use and adaptation of their critical intelligence to the problems of this world. Teachers should also master these processes, infuse them into every lesson every day, and extend them whenever and wherever possible.

PART TWO

Rebuilding for Critical Thinking

Our ability to think, to conceptualize, and to remain open to environmental inputs is clearly limited by the presuppositions of our culture and our times. These assumptions, entrenched in tradition and sanctified by time, also limit the ways in which it is permissible to think. As ingenious as we human beings are, with our highly facile, flexible brain, we are limited by our ability to understand the world around us as well as our own interpretations of that world.

Each person comes to a reality image in his/her own unique way and in terms of personal and cultural limitations and strengths. Within the classroom, the teacher brings to teaching an understanding of the world vastly different than the understandings brought to learning by each individual student. Behind each student there is a variety of orientations/presuppositions, each screaming for absolute status and each demanding that humans live accordingly.

Rebuilding for critical thinking *(RCT)* assumes these differences, these varieties, because each person has been reared within a different cultural context. *RCT* also makes a plea for mental flexibility and openness. We know that each person must make certain philosophic commitments in order to function in his/her environment. Our plea is for commitment without encapsulation, for a person will perish mentally if his/her reality image becomes frozen.

So far as we know, the human brain is the only brain which is aware of itself. In human beings this self-awareness has inevitably led, from generation to generation, to the asking of profound and unyielding questions about life, meaning and the universe. When teachers begin teaching-for-thinking, they and their students will be able to break free from their mental capsules, utilize their growing self-awareness, and face—with a renewed mental vitality—the tough issues and problems challenging them, perhaps more productively. The search for understanding and meaning through thinking will assist us in solving our problems as we continue to break free of thinking that is rigid and frozen to a single point of view.

Because of the very great forces of fragmentation in contemporary life, we need to explicitly exert ourselves toward providing educational situations where integration of knowledge can be maximally fostered and where the student's mind is engaged rather than unengaged in the application of knowledge to pressing human problems. When education reaches the student where he or she lives, it is real, it is powerful, it is meaningful. And while it is true that such an open, thoughtful approach to learning is risky for the student and the teacher in the short view, it is clearly more creative and productive, and, therefore, more viable for all of us in the long run.

Teachers who believe that their task is to educate the Socrates within students can make the classroom a place for asking as well as answering questions.
— Garnet W. Miller, Developing Student Questioning Skills

CHAPTER THREE
Focusing on Concepts

⧼⧽

Any program designed for the teaching-of-thinking will include the study of concepts. Because school subjects are those areas deemed culturally important by our societal traditions and mores, many of the important concepts which we teach will be subject-dependent. These include such concepts as "time," "number," "nation," and "fiction." Other concepts are subject-neutral. These include such concepts as "equality," "knowledge," and "beauty." Therefore, we can easily see that critical thinking will necessarily include concept analysis. A coherent method of conceptual analysis will equip students with a useful tool that can be applied again and again to an ever widening field of knowledge. Conceptual analysis provides a specialized and appropriate method for answering many of the most important and perplexing questions of human living.

Despite the recent interest and new importance placed on *concept-learning*, too many of our students remain concept deficient and factually oriented. Although we mention concepts while teaching, and students apparently can name them and give them rudimentary meanings, too few of them are able to apply familiar concepts to new or similar situations. Most students should be taught concepts related to particular subjects and how these concepts are used and applied in different fields of inquiry. It is a mistake to assume that the understanding of basic concepts seeps automatically into the student's mind. Teaching which focuses on concept-learning will improve communication skills, understanding of subject matter—its application and importance—and student performance. To understand how to teach for conceptual understanding, we need to review the cognitive development of the child in relationship to concept capacity.

HOW CHILDREN LEARN WHAT THEY KNOW

When addressing the question "How do children learn?" Frank Smith (1986) reminds us that the practical issue here is "not so much what children can do without school as what schools must respect if they are to ensure that every child has the opportunity to become literate." In the book, *Awakening to Literacy* (1984), the editors have reached the conclusion "that children learn about using written language from the people around them, from the way those people themselves use written language." Their points of agreement are:

1. All children learn constantly. Children are always striving to understand the form, as well as the function, of the world they are discovering. They hypothesize, change their mind, and generally are able to separate words from other forms of written communication. Children not only learn the kinds of things they see others do with written language, but also explore new usages for words and forms of expression. They are developing a world of literacy all the time. What they are immediately able to do are the things they see being done by other people around them.

From a very early age, children utilize their mind with their senses to operate on their perceived universe in very personal ways. They are sensing the world they experience with **meaning**, and *it is through meaning that conceptual images of the world are generated, revised, compared, thrown out, and/or utilized.* For these reasons, critical thinking and concept analysis originate as natural ways in which children think. We should not view children as miniature and defective users of adult language, because they—like us—work out language for themselves. The tendency of early schooling is to suppress these seemingly natural learning styles and replace them with rote learning, textbooks and measurable goal-oriented subject/skills processing. The language of concepts comes from individual intentions and intelligence rather than from outside manipulation (especially from so-called "thinking skill programs" that are inconsistent with and do not validate the child's natural learning styles and mental abilities). Early on, the teacher's task is to tap into the child's partially filled reservoir of experiences, meanings, intentions and abilities, and there set the stage for a lifetime of learning.

2. Children learn what others do. Children, even those from educationally depressed homes, almost invariably know something about what the written words that appear in television commercials say. They know about the writing on cans and wrappers, on doors, and in stores. Smith says:

> Yetta Goodman, a teacher and education professor from the University of Arizona at Tucson, told the Victoria Symposium that in 5,000 attempts it had proved impossible to find a four-year-old child in the United States who could not read the word McDonalds. I believe that not one of the children thought the word was Muh-Cuh-Doh-Oh-Nuh-Ah-Luh-Duh-Suh, trying to "sound out" the individual letters, though many of them thought it said "hamburgers." But isn't that what the word means?

Children learn language and concepts from the way people in their community use written and spoken language. Margaret Meek (1982) also emphasizes this point. She reminds us:

> …children are natural learners and well disposed to discover for themselves many of the things they need to know. Parents are natural teachers when they share with their children activities they themselves have mastered and enjoy. Good teachers never underestimate the ability of children to learn, nor overestimate the part they play in the process.

Concept-learning and concept-teaching should, therefore, become a natural part of the teaching-for-thinking process. Children pick up concepts from their environment and learn best when everyday experiences are used in the classroom. Chomsky (1959) reminded us that the language of children is too rich, too complex, to be regarded as "habit-learning." His research demonstrated that "sentences grow from entire meanings, from complete intentions, not one word at a time." Concept learning should flow naturally from the subject matter of the schools as this subject matter—as well as the teacher—becomes more and more sensitive to the motivations, intentions and experiences of the children who are the recipients of instruction.

The unnatural methods devised by the behaviorists under the name of "programmed instruction" are elaborately packaged and expensively promoted. They offer carefully prescribed learning sequences, together with workbooks, activity sheets, teacher manuals and tests. In these programs, every skill is clearly defined so there is never any guesswork about what should be done and why. Every lesson is beautifully sequenced and systematic. Within the covers of these materials, learning is promoted as "fun." Together with assessment packages which range from fill in the blanks, circle the correct answer, and go back if you do not get it right, the emphasis is not on meaningful reading and comprehension. Rather, reading for meaning is always supplementary to repetitive skills instruction and is usually accompanied by numerically evaluated questions. Comprehension is also reduced to a set of questions on which students are drilled and tested.

Teaching-for-thinking must break away from the canned, unnatural and measured approach to learning. This is especially true for teaching concepts. Because concepts flow from meanings which come from real experiences, the emphasis should instead focus on getting students to talk and write about their world and to inquire more deeply about those aspects of their experiences that puzzle them. We must trust teachers to teach-for-thinking in their own natural ways and trust also that students will appreciate and learn in a non-threatening and motivating environment, one that gathers from them experiences to write, talk and think about. Furthermore, as we focus on meaning and understanding, we must also develop a multicultural understanding of our students. We must strive to accept the meanings children bring to school in non-threatening way, to understand them, take these meanings into consideration as we plan instructional activities.

3. Children learn what makes sense to them. Smith (1986) says:

> ...children may temporarily be wrong in some of their ideas about what written language does and about how it works. They learn by testing their own hypotheses about language, making sense of it in their own terms. Preschool children's ideas about literacy are never nonsensical. The ideas always make sense, to the child at least; the ideas are always reasonable possibilities. It is not until they get to school that children ever get the idea that reading and writing might

not make sense. And it is not until they get to school that they are confronted with examples of written language and with reading and writing activities that are sheer nonsense. How can you learn from something you do not understand? At school they are often tested to find out what confuses them, and the instruction then concentrates upon that.

Children will learn what makes sense to them. We learn from philosopher E. A. Burtt that insight, meaning and understanding come gradually and require our careful attention. He makes three important observations:

1. The world of the child is the world of common sense—the world they meet in everyday situations.
2. As children learn, their common sense world is continually being modified. Teachers affect directly the knowledges, values, meanings and understandings of their students.
3. Because all knowledge is grounded in common sense, children will use common sense to evaluate new information. Even as their common sense understandings are modified through education, these new meanings will be used to judge and estimate the value of future educational inputs.

Teaching-for-thinking does not have to be prepackaged and artificial. Rather, it can tap into the natural learning styles of students, focus on their basic presuppositions (ideas and concepts generated by common sense experiences), and use these as a base for the search for more accurate images of life and the future. As educators, our quest for a better method of instruction has possibly overlooked the obvious—to possess a method is to have a way of deciding what questions may sensibly be raised, and how to progress toward definite answers, and this method demands that we be able to get inside and outside of ourselves, our culture and our time. The point is that flexibility, both in terms of teaching method and providing a variety of hypotheses, is extremely important. There is not one approach to teaching-for-thinking or for teaching conceptually. The wide variety of intellectual, personality and cultural factors which are involved in learning—both critically and creatively—is the storehouse of our methods. Only recently have we begun to uncover this storehouse.

COGNITIVE DEVELOPMENT AND CONCEPTUAL CAPACITY

Perceptual and Organizational Structures

The principles and skills in the *K-3 Effective Thinking Skills Model* (chapter one, page 24) illustrate the importance of concept learning. From kindergarten to well into the first grade, students are moving from preoperational thinking and learning to the concrete operational stage. During this time, the two organizing principles that define student thinking are (1) the development of skills based on **perceiving**, including learning patterns, relationships, and concepts tied to concrete experiences; and (2) the development of those skills needed for **organizing** the environment, including the skills of classifying, seriating and sequencing. The skills of perceiving and organizing what is perceived, as indicated by part three of the *ETSM Chart*, are based on concept relations and interactions. *Perceptional and organizational structure are the foundation of concept-building, understanding and meaning.*

G. S.. Klein and his associates (1951) observed that *perception* "is the point of reality contact, the door to reality appraisal, and there is no doubt that here especially are the selective adaptive controls of personality brought into play." They reveal that children test their conceptual understandings in three different ways which are keys to the child's organization of reality and subsequent development of understanding.

The first way (leveling versus sharpening of differences) refers to the child's willingness to bring out or ignore differences in what is perceived and understood. The child may be willing to focus on the differences of what is held in common sense and what is now being learned, sharpen these differences and remain open to new information. This is what Piaget called *accommodation*. This child is an aggressive learner and does not retreat from the "outside" world.

The second way (resistance to or acceptance of instability) refers to the child's resistance of or acceptance of ambiguities in new knowledge. If new information is not explained by word and example, the child is likely to be confused and resist learning. If explanation and example are given, the child is more likely to accept temporary confusions and mental instability knowing that the teacher will provide more information so that accommodation is able to occur.

Finally, children will use judging and literal attitudes to test new information. Literal attitudes will assimilate bits and pieces of new information into the understanding with little change being made in the child. What is inconsistent with common sense is simply ignored and what is not is assimilated into established meaning-patterns. If the child is disturbed by new knowledges, s/he may become emotionally involved and highly judgmental. Teaching-for- thinking will enable the student to become better at evaluating or judging new information and using it in future learning situations.

Klein's research into how children learn is important to teaching-for-thinking. He has reminded us that the ability to think critically will enable students to sharpen differences in information, accept temporary confusions and mental instability, and become better at judging anew information and applying it successfully to learning and life situations. Perception is the point where the child's mind begins to interact with his or her environment of people, places, things, situations and ideas. Although this environment is, for the child, concrete (its meanings being entrenched in common sense), it is continually changing. Change will normally cause modifications in understanding and meaning.

Also important to concept development is *organization*. Mental development, the learning process, the culture in which we have developed, and especially the process of perception are all involved in how the child organizes his or her environment. Joseph R. Royce (1964) suggests that *how* a person organizes or structures his or her environment is the key to the development of meaning. This is important for concept understanding. Royce says that if there is organization and differentiation, then there is meaning. On the other hand, if the child merely assimilates new information into old concepts without developing new understandings, then there is homogeneity with few new concepts being developed.

Piaget (1954) believed the concept of structure pervades all thought, from the first sensory-cortical input of the infant to the unified field theory of the physicist. In a lifetime series of experimental research on the thought processes of the child, he demonstrated the importance of **mental structures** for reacting to the external environment. For example, he pointed out that new objects presented to the infant by the external environment can only be responded to in terms of a "mental structure" that has to do with sucking, looking or grasping. Thus, if presented with a one hundred dollar bill, the infant would be more likely to stuff it in his or her mouth than in his or her pocket. The child's "internal structure," essentially sucking, looking or grasping, simply does not include the economic evaluating structure of the adolescent or the adult.

Piaget also demonstrated the importance of internal structuring as a determinant of the ability of children to make a proper induction when exposed to a standard problem. Take, for example, the problem of determining the number of eggs and egg cups under each of three conditions: (1) placing an egg opposite each cup, (2) crowding the eggs into a small space as opposed to stretching out the display of cups, and (3) reversing the latter situation. Piaget found that when the eggs were placed opposite the cups, the children concluded that there were as many eggs as cups, but whatever was bunched together in a small place was seen as fewer in number. The point is that the qualitative level of the response is dependent upon the developmental level (mental structure) of the child.

The Piagetian concepts of assimilation and accommodation are relevant. These two processes are the major ways children adapt to and structure their world. These are the process keys to other conceptual meanings and understandings. **Assimilation** is the process of relating the new to the present cognitive structure of the person. **Accommodation** means the necessity of responding to the new by a change in the present structure of the person. Whereas assimilation is essentially conserving and ego-centered, accommodation is essentially radical and object-centered. Adapting to the world involves a balanced interaction of assimilating and accommodating behaviors. During the younger years the child proceeds primarily by way of assimilation, meeting basic needs rather directly and with little or no awareness of being separate from his or her immediate environment. At this stage the child is not ready for the fine discriminations which the process of accommodation will foster. Mental structure is more rigid and instinctive, allowing for a shallow awareness of the environment.

As the child develops psychobiologically, and as the demands of the environment increase, more and more accommodations become necessary. As the accommodations become more effective, the originally antagonistic interplay between assimilation and accommodation is replaced by feelings of comfortableness and mutuality. These feelings lead the child to an increased facility for taking in more and more of the outside world. Conceptual understandings now become less subjective and more objective. Piaget sees the latter as reflecting a more mature "mental structure."

Perhaps the most interesting aspect of Piaget's work on conceptual structure is the parallel he sees between one's personal "mental structure" and the scientists' theoretical structure of the universe. In the following example, Piaget (1954) describes the child's and the scientist's conception of space:

> The sky seems to us as a big spherical or elliptical cover on whose surface move images without depth which alternately interpenetrate and detach themselves: sun and moon, clouds...It is only through patient observations relating the movements of these images and the way they mask each other, that we arrive at the kind of elaborating subjective groups which satisfied mankind until the constitution of objective groups was made possible by the Copernican image of the earth and the solar system. At first, with regard to immediate perception, there exist neither conscious groups nor permanent solids (the celestial bodies seen to be reabsorbed into each other and not to hide behind one another), nor even depth; there is only accommodation of eyes, head, and body which enables us to follow the movement of some cloud or of the moon, or to perceive a faint star, but the practical groups which we thus utilize are not yet extended into any subjective group...The child's whole space considered from the point of view of distances is analogous to the celestial space of immediate perception which we have just described: a fluid man without depth...transversed by images which interpenetrate or become detached without laws and alternately separate and reunite,...

A comparable situation occurs for the young child as s/he interacts with objects in the external environment and particularly as s/he develops a need to communicate such representations to others. Piaget suggests that a similar evolution from sensorimotor to conceptual thought occurs with other major variables of life such as causality and time. Piaget's (1954) evidence drove him to suggest that

> ...the (child's) completion of the objective practical universe resembles Newton's achievements as compared to the egocentrism of Aristotelian physics, but the absolute Newtonian time and space themselves remain egocentric from the point of view of Einstein's relativity because they envisage only one perspective on the universe among other perspectives, which are equally possible and real.

It is necessary, then, that we understand the developmental patterns of cognitive maturation as we begin the process of concept teaching (teaching for understanding and meaning). From Piaget we learn that all thought starts with instinctive-like assimilation and moves on to an egocentric accommodation, primarily in terms of personal affect (see Klein's three tests of conceptual understandings above) rather than "objective truth." In its advanced stages, the subject-object distinction becomes clearer, the necessity for everything revolving around "me" becomes less and less plausible, and a less egocentric worldview finally emerges. It is important to remember that concept development begins with perception and that "mental structure" (as it develops) tends to order the environment, the perceptual field and the processes of the brain. As we mature, we begin to internalize cultural concepts, understandings and meanings. The culture, which is subsequently internalized gradually, becomes a conceptual ideology ("mental model," see chapter one), a theoretical framework through which we view the world.

Stages of Cognitive Growth

A brief summary of concept capability according to Piagetian developmental stages will increase our understanding of concept development and when and how we should introduce certain types of concepts into our teaching. Also, an understanding of concept capability will let us know what to expect and what not to expect from children at various times during their lives. The **sensorimotor period** (birth to two years) is the time the child develops the ability to operate as if the external world were a permanent place, not one whose existence depends upon his or her perceiving it. As the child approaches two years, a lost object will now be searched for and by different routes. The child now exhibits some idea about his or her surrounding space that permits taking a variety of paths to the same point. Although by age two, the child is able to become goal-directed and shows evidence of purposeful behavior, there are still some serious problems due to a lack of conceptual schemes that correspond to behavioral ones. The child's behavior is very concrete despite its adaptivity, and this concreteness seriously limits how far ahead the child can plan a sequence of actions.

The **preoperational period** (two to seven years) is a time in which the child's internal cognitive picture of the external world with its many laws and relationships is gradually growing. It begins in a piecemeal fashion and gradually the conceptual schemas become organized into interrelated systems which Piaget calls operational. This term implies that the internal actions are now being related by the laws of groups or groupings. When this happens, the child has reached the period of concrete operations. During the preoperational period, the child is painfully unequilibrated in his or her conceptual thinking. The child falls into obvious self-contradictions without quite realizing that the two are incompatible. This period can be puzzling to understand, but it should be thought of as a period of transition in which the child's conceptual ability can be easily over-or under-estimated.

The stage of **concrete operations** (seven to eleven years) is a time when the child's formal thought processes become much more stable and reasonable. Objects can now be arranged in order and new ones placed into the series. The child can understand that equality of number of two sets of objects depends upon a one-to-one correspondence between the objects in the two groups. The child understands that the number of objects in a group is not changed by purely spatial rearrangements. Classes of objects and their relations can now be understood. A rudimentary conception of time, space, number and logic—those fundamental conceptions in terms of which our understanding of events and objects is ordered—can now be grasped.

Formal operations (beginning at age eleven) is also a time of transition in which the child begins to understand the basic principles of causal thinking and scientific experimentation. An understanding of the scientific method—which consists of holding control variables constant while varying one experimental variable at a time—is now beginning to cognitively mature. Experiments can be performed and conclusions deduced, at least in some instances. Beginning at this stage (around grades six and seven), teachers can introduce science, math and history fairs as a tool for introducing formal thinking. These programs enable teachers to introduce formal thinking processes into the curriculum in a way that motivates and stimulates the student to learn.

DEFINITIONS AND EXPLANATIONS

Two problems have traditionally been associated with teaching concepts. First, experience has shown that many teachers are still unclear about what they think a concept is. Facts, concepts, values and skills should be included in every lesson every day, but we must also understand that these categories represent different levels of meaning and understanding of human experience. When students are able to explain the relationship of these terms and processes, their understanding will be increased and their schooling improved. Concept-learning is a basic and essential process.

Second, another reason for the inadequate teaching of concepts may be the assumption that concepts are learned in the same way that facts, values, and skills are learned. There are many different methods of processing information, and the processing of concepts has its own methodology. When we do not understand and use this method adequately, we cannot be sure that students understand or are able to use essential concepts. The method of conceptual analysis presented in this chapter provides a framework to thinking which might otherwise meander indefinitely, without direction, among the many avenues of intellect and culture. Students need to spend less time collecting facts and accepting teacher biases uncritically and more time learning how to analyze, synthesize and evaluate the informational inputs that are the result of in-school and out-of-school learning.

Although concepts occur naturally in the vocabulary of young children, we must help them clarify, utilize and extend these meanings to their growing experiences and to an ever widening field of intellectual inquiry. In teaching-for-thinking, a part of the teacher's role will be to determine if students can use concepts consistently in both familiar and unfamiliar situations and whether they can use them when making comparisons for similarities and differences. One of the major functions of concept-learning is the metaphorical use of concepts in situations that call for explanation. The use of metaphor will also add depth and richness to the language of science. In most cases, it will enrich ordinary language as well, adding to our explanations and descriptions mental pictures that extend meaningful thought (requiring one to use the imagination, visual imagery and/or fantasy).

Definitions

When working with students to clarify and extend the use of their conceptual knowledge, the teacher is required to make certain distinctions in ordinary language. It will do no good to require students to memorize these categories. Their consistent use in teaching/learning situations is enough to quicken the awareness and assist students with understanding their environments. The following five distinctions will assist concept learning:

1. Concept: A set of attributes common to any and all: instances of a given class, type, kind and category.
2. Example: Any and all individual items that have the characteristics of a given concept.
3. Nonexample: Any and all individual items that may have some but not all of the characteristics of a given concept.
4. Concept-label: One or more terms (names) used to refer to any and all examples of a given concept. The concept is the set of characteristics, not the label.
5. Fact: Verifiable information about an individual item, whereas a concept is a generalization in a person's mind about what is true of any and all items (facts) that are examples of the same class.

Explanations

1. All concepts are abstract. Concepts are mental patterns—groups of characteristics—of concrete specific examples. The actual characteristics of individual items (particular instances or examples of a concept) may be either concrete or symbolically represented. These symbolic representations may be concrete (a road sign is a concrete representation of the intersection that lies ahead) or abstract (the idea of beauty, which is mental, may represent a concrete object or person). Young children rely on concrete representations and base their conceptualizations upon them. The characteristics of a concrete example are directly perceivable to them through their senses. They rely on these perceptual processes to formulate conceptual images and are able to organize their experiences and environment through them. At the rudimentary level, children formulate concepts by their concrete interactions with their environment.

For example, a preoperational or early concrete operational child may be asked to draw a picture of four different kinds of chairs. Most older students will have no problem with this. The concept chair is in their minds. They understand and are able to apply this knowledge to the teacher's directions. Each drawing represents a particular chair which they may have experienced. Younger children may not have the experiences or the abstract ability to "pull" these drawings from their experiences. The drawing is symbolic. It is concrete but comes from an interaction of awareness and memory, making it an abstract process. Once completed, the drawing is also concrete. Still, it remains more abstract than the actual chairs that were formally experienced. Being able to identify the concept of chair and then group characteristics of the many items of this single class into an example or representation tells the teacher that students have an understanding of the concept under consideration.

2. Concepts cannot be verified. Only facts (propositions which are complete statements about individual perceptions) can be verified. For example, "I see the ball," or, "The green ball is on the desk," are factual statements. Using perceptual experiences, these statements can be determined as true or false, right or wrong. On the other hand, concepts do not represent facts about the world; they are categorizations of facts (abstract groupings). Whether Johnny can carry out the directive, "Johnny, please draw a picture of a ball," depends on whether he "holds" in his mind the conception of "ball." When learning a concept, the student is actually learning the characteristics of the concept, not particular instances of it.

3. Concepts are hierarchical. Some concepts include other concepts. They depend on each other for their meaning. Another way of saying this is to remind ourselves that some concepts have meanings that are interrelated. For example, the concept of *living thing* includes *plants* and *animals*. *Animals* include *vertebrates* and *invertebrates*. The same pattern holds for social and philosophical concepts as well. Teaching the concept of *equality* will include other concepts such as *fairness, nondiscrimination* and *love.* Here the teacher will also employ word opposites (and concept opposites) to enrich understanding and concept application.

TECHNIQUES OF ANALYSIS

There are some general considerations which are nearly always useful and which one should apply whenever faced with any question involving conceptual analysis.

Isolated Questions of Concept

As teachers, we must insist that students identify concepts as concepts. Only rarely will a person be presented with a question of concept in its pure form. Consider the following two questions:

1. What is the logical nature of the concept of "punishment?"
2. Should people in mental institutions ever be punished?

Clearly, the first question is a question of concept in its pure form, but most people do not ask this question. They will ask questions similar to the second example, questions in which concept identification is more confused and complex.

To answer the second question, students (or teachers) must first recognize that *punishment* is the concept under scrutiny and proceed to identify its major characteristics. Secondly, they must have or gather some factual information of what kind of people are in mental institutions, and, finally, they must express some sort of opinion about whether punishment is properly applied to these people.

In other words, the second example is a mixed question of the type most teachers and students will ask and involves not only conceptual analysis but considerations of a factual and, possibly, a moral sort as well. It may not be your teaching purpose to answer the above questions of fact and value with regard to the second question. It is clear no answer will be dearly and consistently stated at all unless the student and teacher are able to distinguish between the differing types of questions concealed within what looks like a single question.

"Right Answers"

There can be no "right answer" to the whole mixed question like number two above. This is why the question of concept needs to be isolated from other considerations and dealt with first. Questions of fact and value cannot relevantly be applied at all until one has worked out just what they are supposed to be applied to—in this case, the concept of "punishment."

One should be careful to state concepts in terms of the set of characteristics by which the examples are identified and distinguished from nonexamples. Several clear examples and nonexamples of the concept need to be used. For example, if one main characteristic of "punishment" is *being subject to a penalty or to pain because of some offense*, then certainly one who steals or hurts another person should be punished. But when we add to this concept the characteristic of *being responsible for one's actions*, then it is really not clear whether people in mental institutions should ever be punished. When isolating the question of concept, one must decide—through examples and nonexamples—what are the essential characteristics of the concept under consideration. The teacher must be careful with application and sensitize students to the context of usage. It is this sort of sensitivity that makes all the difference between a useful and successful analysis and a clumsy attempt to analyze the concept merely by listing its instances without distinguishing between them.

Model Cases

What is useful in concept teaching is to choose a "model case." A model case is an example of a concept which one feels completely sure is an instance of the concept. For example, returning to the concept of "punishment," we could use the example of a student who willfully and purposefully sets fire to the school and was severely punished for the crime. There was no question about who set the fire, since the student was caught in the act of setting it. There was no question about the student's intentions. The student admitted setting the fire because s/he was angry at a particular teacher for the low grades s/he received during the last report period. This seems to be an example of a model case for the concept of "punishment."

As we consider this case, we should determine the essential characteristics of the concept "punishment." We might reason it is a fact the student actually broke the law by setting fire to the school; or the student willfully (is responsible for h/her actions) broke the law; or s/he was caught in the act; or s/he was dealt with by authorities; or some combinations of these.

From this analysis, teachers should assist their students with the creation of other model cases, either actual examples or ones which we or our students can imagine. These new examples will help students understand the essential features of the concept. Were the essential features of the first example also present in the second and third examples? If not, are they essential or nonessential to our analysis? Essential features will be present in all model cases of the concept. By this procedure, we can help students narrow the search for the essential features of a concept while eliminating the nonessential ones.

Nonexamples or Contrary Cases

An opposite method can also be used to identify the essential characteristics of a concept. This can be accomplished by taking cases of which we are able to say, "Well, whatever so-and-so is, this certainly is not an example of it."

If the concept under examination is that of "justice," we would pick some cases about which we would definitely say that a person was being treated *unjustly*. Suppose an innocent student is accused of setting fire to the school and sent to a juvenile home for the crime. Suppose two people commit the same crime under the same circumstances, and one is punished while the other is set free. We might conclude that these are cases of injustice which are **nonexamples** of "justice."

But what makes these model cases? In the second example, when the law treated two people differently, it appears that the essential feature is inequality or unfairness. Is it because the two people are not treated the same way that we call the situation "unjust?" We must remember that there are cases which appear to be the same but, upon careful analysis, have essential characteristics that differ.

Borderline Cases

Many of the examples and nonexamples used by students will be borderline cases. As we move through the problems associated with conceptual analysis, it will be helpful to assist students with the examination of these particular kind of cases. Borderline cases are those where we are not sure; they are usually vague, confusing or based on unclear examples. Suppose a child touches an electric wire which s/he has repeatedly been told not to touch and then gets badly burned. Is the shock and resultant burn "punishment" (going back to our first concept)? Is it deserved? Also, when we talk about a professional boxer "taking plenty of punishment," are we serious in using the word "punishment" here, or are we using it as a metaphor? Again, can a person bring punishment upon him/herself or must punishment be delivered by someone else? The point is to elucidate the nature of the concept by continually facing different cases which lie on the borderline of our understanding of its essential and nonessential characteristics.

The Pitfalls of Language

Many problems associated with the clarification and understanding of concepts are subtle and disguised. They are due to the nature of language. We fall into these traps for one fundamental reason—we are dominated and bewitched by the language that we use. We allow words to guide our thinking instead of consciously and critically using thinking to choose the words and concepts which we employ. The analysis of concepts will be aided by avoiding the following language pitfalls.

Pitfall: Belief in Abstract Objects. This is a pitfall of language which is difficult to avoid. For example, Mrs. Smith teaches language arts at the fourth grade level in her school. Many of her students are in Mrs. Laney's social studies class. In language arts, Mrs. Smith teaches that abstract concepts are to be treated grammatically as nouns. She tells her class that, as nouns, abstract concepts can be verified as facts. Mrs. Laney, on the other hand, teaches social studies and focuses much attention on such abstract concepts as "justice," "nation," and "government." She concludes that these concepts may be treated as nouns but that they are not objects like chairs, houses, and boats. Object-nouns can be perceived by the senses and statements about them and verified as true or false by utilizing perception. Statements embodying concept-nouns cannot be verified as true or false by the senses. They can only be explained, understood and applied in the context of usage.

Abstract concepts do not exist in the perceivable world. They are generalizations from experience and serve—abstractly—to organize our thinking and clarify our understanding of relationships and patterns which are perceived in the observable world. The thing itself—a particular chair, house or boat—is perceivable and verifiable. The concept that holds in our meaning the idea of chair, house or boat is unperceivable and, hence, unverifiable.

Pitfall: Confusion of Fact and Value. Many questions we ask are mixed questions; that is, they demand both conceptual analysis and a value judgment. Such words as "good," "bad," "right," "wrong," "ought," and "should" are expressions of value. Their function is to prescribe, approve, condemn, praise or blame. Other words such as "honesty," "stealing," "noble," and "just" have both a factual and a value meaning. They refer to certain kinds of behavior which can be perceived. Hence, they are factual. They also imply a value judgment—a judgment of approval or disapproval.

Teachers who coach for thinking skill improvement and conceptual development need to become more sensitive to concept-labels, their context of usage, and their logical implications. Many times textbooks do not point out these differences, and they may even confuse fact and value themselves. If the teacher is aware that they exist, s/he will be able to create lessons and learning opportunities to enhance their explanations and understandings.

Pitfall: Unseen Implications. Also, some words have unseen implications. These implications reflect the "mental models" both teachers and students bring to the learning environment. Consider the following question: "Have you stopped kicking your dog today?" This question has unseen implications and, for the unknowing person, is a mental trap. If a person answers "Yes" to this question, then this implies that "s/he *has been* kicking his or her dog." If the person answers "No" to this question, then this implies that "s/he has been kicking his or her dog and continues to do it."

Some older students might be interested in the concept of "self." They will at times say to a friend or to a teacher: "I'm just not myself today." Of course, if a person is not himself or herself, then who can s/he be? A person cannot be someone else? Critical thinking will deal with small meanings which have unseen implications because these can cause confusion. Clarity and understanding are the goals of concept teaching.

TEACHING FOR CONCEPT UNDERSTANDING

In their book, *Study Skills in the Content Areas* (1982), Askov and Kamm remind us that "skills instruction can best be described as having two phases: development and application. During the development phase, the teacher usually introduces a skill that he or she has determined the students do not know and then familiarizes them with different aspects of it." The **development phase** of instruction will usually involve a sample task from reading materials, the textbook or other materials that the students are using. If the purpose is to teach or coach for skill/concept proficiency, then it is best to focus on one skill at a time, independent of other skills that the teacher may want to teach. The easiest use of the skill should be taught first, followed by more sophisticated uses.

Even when dealing with **concept clusters**—concept clusters are groups of concepts that share similar meanings or several major characteristics; i.e., "city," "town," "village," and "community" represent a concept cluster—it is important to focus on one concept at a time. When the concept is linked to other similar concepts, the teacher should sequence the learning activities in order to avoid confusion, allowing stu-

> Being sure that students learn concepts thoroughly—even to the point of reviewing the other prerequisite concepts (concepts that have been previously taught)—aids retention and helps them apply the concept and integrate it with other concepts later on.

dents to understand the concept tagged for this part of the lesson before moving on to more complicated concepts in the hierarchy. As a rule of thumb, teaching the simplest concept first will make learning easier, because its meaning will be included in the meaning of the more complex concept. For example, the meaning of "village" ("a small assemblage of houses in a country district, larger than a hamlet and generally smaller than a town, and sometimes incorporated as a municipality") is a part of the meaning of "town" ("a collection of inhabited houses generally larger than a village and having more complete local government, but less elaborate than a city").

In the **application phase** of instruction, the main emphasis is on students' independent use of the concept they have learned. The same concept will be used in a variety of subjects, materials and classes. Meanings will normally vary depending on context. In the application phase, students should be encouraged to create examples, non-examples, model cases, contrary cases, and borderline cases of the concept. Careful attention to the application of concept knowledge will increase both student understanding and analytical ability.

Because of the pressures of time and coverage of materials, we sometimes do not give enough attention to the application of concept knowledge. Although we may believe that students have mastered a skill or a concept during instruction or because they have passed an objective test in which the concept was used, giving them a chance to apply the skill or concept in a real-life situation will enrich their knowledge and enhance their understanding. It is important for teachers to provide both development and application instruction for their students. The lesson plan guide (chapter one, page 16) encourages the application phase of instruction in its third section, "Feedback Correctives," which is used for both re-teaching and mastering and enrichment for the entrenchment of skills and concepts.

The following three techniques will help get you started with concept skill instruction:

Isolate the conceptual question or questions from the rest of the materials.

- Unfamiliar vocabulary and concepts should be introduced before extensive reading and application activities are assigned.
- Write down the concept or concepts to be analyzed.
- Apply the techniques of developing model cases, contrary cases, and borderline cases to the concept.
- An abundance of practice materials should be used. Demonstrate and apply the concept in different contexts. A single exposure to the concept will not produce permanent learning. Repeated exposures will emphasize the importance of the concept and highlight its meaning.
- Have students write on paper the significant meanings of the concept. Have them write the insignificant meanings.
- Students should be encouraged to think aloud to a friend about the meaning of the concept. They should tell their friends the significant characteristics of the concept and have their friends ask them questions for clarity and understanding.
- Students should also be encouraged to invent new cases and apply them to the model cases discussed during the development phase. They should review their work and be encouraged to amend any remarks that seem out of place or mistaken.

Enhance concept development through concept-mapping. Mapping is a visual representation of the essential characteristics of a concept. These relationships, when demonstrated visually, will be particularly helpful in understanding the meaning of a passage. When mapping a concept, place the concept-label in the center with other characteristics or relationships represented visually around it. For example, the visual picture of the concept of "community" will help young students see its significant features:

On occasion, students will become confused because two or more concepts share significant characteristics. This confusion can also be

Figure 3.1: Visual Picture of the concept of "Community"

A social group	Having location	Organized, shared government

COMMUNITY

Common beliefs, history	Similar interests	Small village or town

overcome by mapping. A visual picture of concept relationships will strengthen the students' understanding and decrease mistakes. For example, a student might be confused about the significant differences between *"town"* and *"city."* Examples one and two can be utilized to demonstrate the significant similarities and differences of these two concepts.

Other representations of the same material are possible. The teacher should encourage the creativity of each student by having him or her devise visual representations of important concepts and ideas. This will

Example One

Characteristics of "Town"	Shared Characteristics	Characteristics of "City"

Example Two

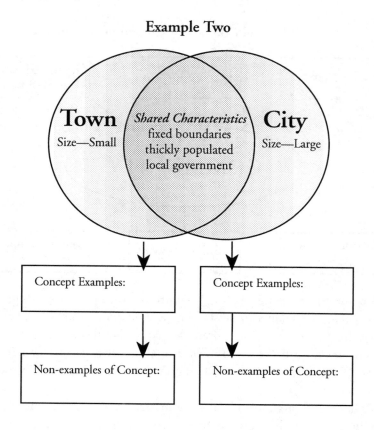

Example Three

> ### Instructions for Mapping a Reading Passage:
>
> 1. Read the entire passage before mapping.
> 2. Determine the organization of the passage.
> 3. Write down significant concepts in the passage.
> 4. Mark the important relationships in the passage.
> 5. Write out the model and contrary cases of the concepts.
> 6. Any map that expresses the correct relationship is appropriate.

make the concept more easily remembered not only because the student has a visual representation of the concept, but also because the student has applied time and effort in thinking about the relationships expressed in order to portray the concept- characteristics in a visual map.

Older students—upper elementary, middle school and secondary—should be encouraged to use this technique for comprehending and analyzing important passages in textbooks, novels and other difficult reading materials. Completing a visual map of one's own making will strengthen memory and greatly assist the student with understanding the material being studied.

Having students map a reading passage will also strengthen understanding, comprehension and concept knowledge. Example three can be used by the teacher to fit the age level and material under review.

Fourth or fifth grade students reading *The Whipping Boy* by Sid Fleischman (1986) can be introduced to the concept of "whipping boy" through a development-phase concept lesson. To begin this lesson, the teacher should introduce the book by reading Chapter One to the entire class.

The chapter should be read down to where the king says, "Fetch the whipping boy." The young prince was pictured as a spoiled brat. "Not even black cats would cross his path." In this opening chapter, the prince has tied the wigs of the lords and ladies—attending a feast in the king's castle—to the backs of their chairs. When they stand up, their wigs fly off. No one laughs but the young prince. That is when the king calls for the "whipping boy."

Step One

- To determine the organization of the chapter and book, the teacher should ask students what is going on here.
- Students should be permitted to re-tell the story to this point. They then should be encouraged to speculate about the characteristics of the concept "whipping boy."
- Permit them to map their hypotheses on the chart on the following page.

Step Two:

- Students should then be permitted to read the rest of Chapter One.
- They should be encouraged to write out the actual characteristics of the concept of "whipping boy."
- On their concept map they should then check their hypothesized characteristics against the actual characteristics of this con-

Concept Label: *Whipping Boy*		
Hypothesized Characteristics	Number Correct	Actual Characteristics

Figure 3.2: Map of Contrary Cases

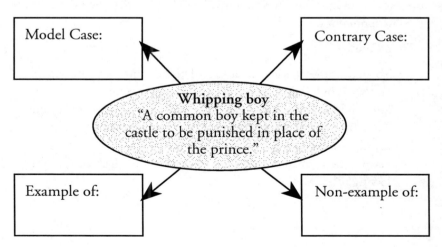

cept and mark with an X those with the same or similar meaning.
- Model and contrary cases of the concept of "whipping boy" can be mapped according to Figure 3.2.

For older students a complete and in depth discussion of lesson concepts, especially those of similar meaning or opposite meaning, is essential. In the following example a short passage has been taken from a *National Geographic* article (Vesilind, 1990) on the Baltic nations. Given is the subtitle and the opening paragraphs of the article. Two concepts seem to jump off the pages, begging for analysis and understanding. These are **independence** and **free man**.

"Estonia, Latvia, and Lithuania struggle toward independence"
The last free man in Estonia was hunted down in 1978 August. Sabe was the sole survivor of the Forest Brothers, men who took to the woods to resist the occupying Soviets in 1944. He was finally found in southern Estonia by two KGB agents posing as fishermen. A photograph shows the 56-year-old Sabe and an agent sitting on a

Figure 3.3: Concept Map

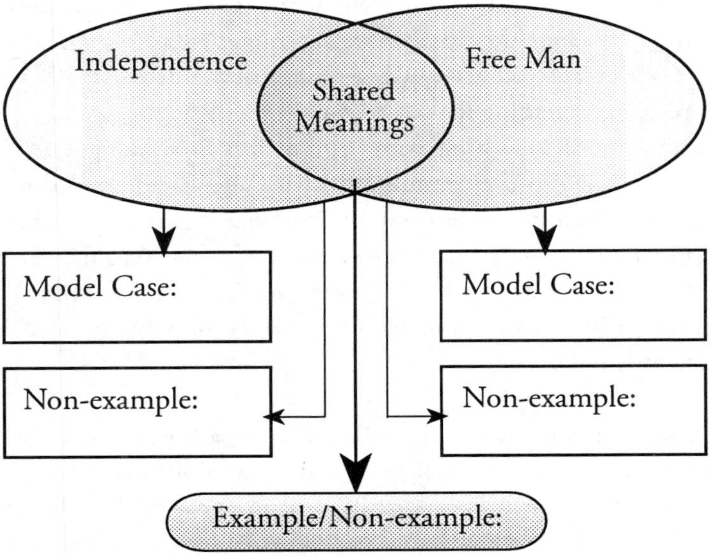

riverbank. Sabe holds a fishing pole and grins for the photographer, the other KGB man. Minutes later they tried to arrest him, and Sabe wrestled one agent into the river. But more agents were on their way, and, seeing no escape, he dived underwater and hooked himself to a submerged log, ending his life.

Develop concept meaning through analysis and discussion. Using mapping in conjunction with concept analysis will help teachers increase student understanding of complex materials. Analysis and discussion will also help students discover more meaning in what they read and study. Students should spend less time simply accepting the concepts and explanations of others uncritically and more time in learning how to analyze concepts in both real life and study situations. The techniques used in this chapter can be of use to students at any grade level and in any situation.

Conceptual analysis is a kind of mental engineering that, when deployed successfully by teachers and learned by students, can elevate the potentialities of the youthful mind. It is a method of clear thought that will promote clearer writing and more complete comprehension. Conceptual analysis can become an effective tool or method by which to judge written materials and verbal arguments. This method is concerned with words and the meanings of statements. It seeks logic and clearness. As we use it, we should become more and more intensely aware that language is not an abstract activity, but a form of life. It is something used by people and something that uses people.

Students continue to bring with them their own meanings and understandings, learned in the community environment and applied in daily living. These "mental models" cry out for analysis and comprehension. Thus, it will not only be to textbooks and school materials that we apply this technique of learning. It will also be applied to the understandings and language brought in to us by our students. As John Wilson (1963) so poignantly reflects:

> With men, however, to have the power of saying "I had a ghastly experience yesterday" is itself to have the power of conscious experience; of being conscious of what happens to one and what one does, of remembering it, naming and describing it, thinking about it and

interpreting it. Man has the freedom to attach, within limits circum-scribed by his own nature, whatever force or weight to his experiences he likes: the freedom to give them meaning.

The analysis of concepts emerges as an important tool for both stu-dent and teacher. It is a necessary tool because it is a good way of gener-ating consciousness. This is important because meaning goes deeper than usage—it comes from our reservoir of conceptual meanings which itself is rooted in our personality and past experiences. It is the sensitivity we give to conceptual meaning that makes all the difference between sur-face learning and learning that can change lives. Conceptual analysis will equip students with a single, coherent technique of thought which they can apply over a wide field in a lifetime of study and learning.

The discussion of ideas and concepts, meanings and conflicting data will greatly assist students understanding more fully and deeply the ma-terials which they study. The Paideia Program, discussed in chapter sev-en, focuses much needed attention on discussion and seminar tech-niques. After teaching basic information to students, after extending and enriching this information through activities and examples, after coach-ing students in thinking skills and processes, the teacher should then en-gage students in discussions of ideas, concepts, assumptions and the im-plications which they have drawn from the study. Only in this way can we actively engage students in their own learning and challenge them at the growing edge of their knowledge.

CHAPTER FOUR

Facilitating Skills (Grades K–3)

ℰℐ

CHILDREN AS NATURAL THINKERS

To survive in an increasingly technical age is largely dependent on our ability to marshal the genius in every person. Perhaps we have undersold the mission of the school. The past decade, with its back-to-basics movement based on hard data from our schools, demonstrated how concerned the public is for skill improvement in the traditional areas of reading, writing, and mathematics (science and social studies were also added to this list). While these efforts are foundational, there is serious concern that many teachers and curricular planners share—the omission of any sense of *coordination* of skills toward a common objective. That is, having defined the purpose of schooling, is there any effort to develop and blend critical thinking and learning skill processes toward a singular goal?

To be sure, skill operations such as problem solving, inquiry and decision making can be infused into basic subject areas and broken into smaller skill units (such as hypothesis formation and inference making) for teaching, blending and utilizing diverse information in humanly useful ways. Too many subject-related skills, critical thinking skills, and skill combinations are being taught in isolation from both content and each other. The result is pedagogical confusion, program fragmentation, and the inefficient use of teaching/learning time.

In chapter one a detailed unfolding of critical thinking skills demonstrated the relationship between skills and skill combinations. This chapter also provided a critical thinking skills continuum linking critical thinking skills to the activity of problem solving. H. M. Hartoonian (1980) points out that a number of curricular objectives, in all subject areas, are "common in their use of 'reasoning rhetoric.'" Within them, he points out, we discover objective-fragments (or sub-objectives) that contain some attributes of reasoning but do not offer a complete, developmentally appropriate strategy for this purpose. He comments:

> If we look at course outlines and subject matter curriculum guides and materials, then it also appears that although the quantities and qualities of discourse modes vary in different disciplines, the kinds of skills required to function adequately in all areas seem to be *common* in that they address reasoning abilities.

The irony is that many educational professionals involved in thinking skill development and improvement cannot agree on the definition and identification of these skills. Also, public school textbooks have either excluded the development of thinking from serious instructional intention or present an unorganized and developmentally inappropriate thinking skills format in their workbooks and teacher guides.

Obviously, we should give serious attention to the development of thinking and reasoning. Torrance (1990) has reminded us that we should perhaps assist students "...enlarge, enrich, and make more accurate their images of the future." Indeed, the search for ideas that make possible the creation of a better world, that help students examine, modify, adapt and elaborate their vision of the future until it becomes uniquely their own, requires the ability to think, reason and solve important human problems.

Let us be reminded that children are natural thinkers and that the ability to reason will develop as a general function of cognitive maturation. Although children do think naturally, within an educational setting the skills of problem solving and critical thinking will not be refined, enriched, or extended without conscious instruction. Peter Langford (1989) observes that "teaching can help children learn about classification/and other skills of thinking/more quickly than if they were left entirely to their own devices." The subtlety, nuance and sharpness of reasoning power and ability do not just happen. A conscious and formal commitment to the teaching of thinking is crucial. Yet, despite many efforts, a careful review of currently available educational materials reveals

> The move from an emphasis on memorization and the evaluation of retained-memories will require a revolution in thinking about teaching.

nearly a complete lack of attention to the structural development of thinking and reasoning skills.

As was pointed out in chapter two, effectively accomplishing this task will require the learning of new skills and skill combinations, the development of tolerance for multiple interpretations, and the ability to explore and create alternatives. Also important to remember is that the emphasis on cognitive growth and refinement is not a separate curriculum which will replace existing subject matter and basic learning skills (reading, writing and mathematics). Rather, thinking skills, when systematically and consistently infused into content and content skill activities, will quicken the pace of learning, as well as enrich and broaden the use of intelligence as it is carefully applied to both school learning and life areas.

For teachers it will take courage to break free from "purely" textbook materials, to redefine knowledge and learning in terms of thinking, and to redevelop teaching strategies and methods for evaluating what is learned and how it learned.

Curricula, in its present departmentalized and compartmentalized form, is the dinosaur of public education. Knowledge gained through experience does not come to students neatly packaged, separated and sequenced. Human beings and their children are introduced to the world as it is. Knowledge, from the human point of view, is the organized understandings (meanings) of our interactions with a world of people, natural events, and social happenings. Knowledge is, therefore, interrelated and complex like the world it mirrors. Knowledge includes facts as well as values, concepts and methods of knowing. Given the complexity of the world (its multiethnic and multicultural nature) and our understandings of it, should we not make as our primary goal the emphasis of learning that requires the use of intelligence and impacts on the inequities and complexities of the real world and not merely the world via textbook images?

Knowledge that cultures thrive when they are continuously transformed through extrapolations from the past and present into the future, guided by a vision of what might be, is essential. Using this idea as a guide, we should be motivated to organize our teaching to include discovery, inquiry and problem solving. Stimulated by this idea, teaching will be organized for interacting with nature and other human beings, extending and elaborating upon what is learned, and infusing learning-thinking processes in every lesson every day.

A developmentally appropriate "skills network" can assist us in moving toward the goal of utilizing the natural thinking abilities of students in positive and "learningful" ways. In this chapter we begin with the primary years and the skills that were identified (in chapter one) as **facilitating skills**. These skills and skill combinations are foundational to the beginning of learning. We certainly know that children in the primary grades are not only able to use these skills artfully, but that teachers should teach these skills to them in order to extend learning and make it more conceptually meaningful. If the goal of formal education is to provide the foundation for students to become life long learners, then thinking and reasoning should be taught along with those content-related skills (reading, math, writing, etc.) that are culturally significant, culture-producing, and multicultural in nature.

FACILITATING SKILLS

1. Background

At the primary level we begin with **facilitating skills** development. This set of skills is foundational to all other thinking processes and, also, to the learning of basic subject matter. Some students will master these skills much more quickly than other students. Discovering that some youngsters are already able to use facilitating skills, even at rudimentary levels, will not be uncommon during the primary years. This should not deter teachers from teaching these skills to all students. Teachers need to make sure that facilitating skills are mastered, refined and applied in a variety of subjects and situations. A common complaint about thinking skills programs is that too many skills are presented at each grade level and teachers are unable to teach all of them effectively. Hartoonian

(1980) has pointed out that when fewer skills are stressed at each grade level, the skills of critical thinking can be organized, developed, and infused into lesson activities more completely and student performance is improved.

Young children enter school already in the process of acquiring the ability to symbolically represent their world in word and thought. They are acquiring elementary reasoning abilities and are beginning to formulate concepts of **classes of objects** and **general relations.** Thinking at this age is based on making careful observations and classifying what is seen in some reliable way. The young child's world is filled with a large and indiscriminate array of different experiences, objects, people, animals and events. Early on in life, the young child tries to impose some sort of order on this bundle of sensations and impressions. Before ages four or five, the child is unable to make graphic collections of these experiences. As yet, the material of experience has not been sorted out and identical items classified (together) in reliable ways.

During the primary years of schooling, the child increasingly feels the need to organize these experiences so that s/he is able to impose some sort of order on the experienced environment. Important to learning is that teachers help the child develop both perceptual and organizing skills. We have noted (chapter one, page 24) that the two organizing principles of primary thinking are (1) **perceptual skills:** sensory learning patterns and their relationship to past experiences; and (2) **organizing skills:** the ability to classify, seriate, and sequence the data of experience. Interestingly, after the age of four and one half years (Langford 1989), there is an enormous advance in classificatory thinking. Children advance from using inconsistent and variable methods of classification to making systematic sorting along a singular dimension. At about the age of seven or eight, children are able to sort (classify) using two criteria. Also, they are able to cope with hierarchical classifications which still cause some difficulty for children at the middle school or junior high school level. However, when taught consistently and systematically at the primary level (Lowell 1980), children are able to learn such systems of classification by the age of nine.

One of the major goals of thinking (and of teaching for thinking skill improvement) is to move away from rough and primitive categories to concepts and definitions that work with greater precision. One of the basic thinking skills associated with perceptual and organizing skill development is that of causality. A careful study of the *Effective Thinking Skills Model, K-3* (chapter one, page 24) reveals a heirarchical rendering of facilitating skills leading to use of cause and effect thinking. Although primary children are incapable of refined causal reasoning, they are capable of more accurate causal reasoning than once believed. As children mature intellectually, their conceptual capacity will continue to refine and enrich causal thinking in meaningful and, perhaps, more accurate ways.

Also during the primary years, there appears to be a basic confusion of **the one and the many.** Concepts representing "the many"—food, vehicles, animals, plants, etc.—and concepts representing specific objects ("the one")—a specific food item, tree, animal, etc.—are sometimes confused. This confusion will affect learning in all subject areas. Thus, the integration of facilitating skills into teaching and learning during the early years of schooling is requisite and necessary for all learning and educational progression. Learning these skills is an antidote to later educational remediation.

The primary years are when students are acquiring the ability to operate upon **symbols** as they learn to organize their world and make simple inferences from their personal experiences. This is a critical period of student growth in cognitive ability, a time which requires skill practice and reinforcement, expansion and refinement. By the middle of the second grade most students are able to classify, understand the concept of number, decode new words, and infer meaning. The ability to manipulate symbols makes possible a whole new level of achievement (Inhelder and Piaget 1964) and opens to the child a new level of understanding.

Children do not think like adults. During the primary years, they begin to carry out operations in their heads such as adding and subtracting, following steps in problem solving, grouping and regrouping, putting events in order, naming the steps in a process, and describing how to get from one place to another. During this time, the teacher may discover that "wholes" and "parts" are still confused and that students are unable to think of several aspects of a situation at once. Piaget (1971/1974) also found that younger children will use a number of unscientific forms of causal thinking. These include the following:

1. **Animism**—The child explains that an object moves because it is alive and has intentions and feelings. ("Clouds run one another across the sky.")
2. **Artificialism**—Natural formations are the result of human construction. ("Seas were dug to put fish in;" and "The moon was placed in the sky for us to see at night.")
3. **Marginal Similarity**—Children explain unrelated events because they resemble one another. ("Rabbits dig holes in the ground because woodpeckers bore holes in trees.")
4. **Transductive Reasoning**—Children go from one aspect of A to the same aspect of B to an aspect of C; therefore A is related to C. ("Trees have sap like humans have blood. Blood is warm and sunlight is warm. Therefore, sap is warm like sunlight.")
5. **Phenomenalism**—If two things regularly happen together, one causes the other, even if they are physically separated and are in fact unrelated. ("Rain comes because the sun goes in.")

Recent research (Langford 1989) has shown that while young children do often use unscientific explanations, they sometimes use scientific types as well. If teachers are prepared to teach to children's strengths rather than their weaknesses, **causal thinking** can certainly be taught to primary children. Therefore, attention needs to be given to the careful construction of learning activities, appropriate questioning techniques, cooperative learning lessons, and metacognitive (feedback) exercises that are able to help students refine and develop their cognitive abilities and mend their cognitive deficiencies.

Teaching-for-thinking requires that primary level teachers give careful attention to the foundational critical thinking principles and the micro-thinking skills which can be generated from them. Emphasis will be placed on generating and clarifying ideas, making accurate observations and utilizing evidence to draw conclusions. The skills of perceiving, classifying, seriating, and sequencing serve as an organizational base from which to generate the other thinking operations associated with facilitating skills. Facilitating skills are the building blocks of higher thought. As the young child leaves the primary grades, s/he is now able to put ideas, as well as objects, in sequence, remember the whole while dividing it into parts, and reverse these operations to return the parts to their original states. The child can now make valid relationships among objects observed, perform experiments, and make rudimentary logical explanations and predictions based on cause/effect relationships.

The growth in the ability to classify and make relationships requires opportunities for observing and manipulating objects. Organizing skills (classifying, seriating and sequencing) lead to concept formation — the ability to group and pattern the universe of experience into larger categories, allowing the creation of definitions that work with greater precision. Finally, facilitating skills allow children the opportunity to develop ideas about causality — the essential ingredient in creating scientific and logical explanations. These skills form the core of developmentally appropriate thinking skills for the primary years. Their mastery is essential if children are to learn to reason abstractly and effectively use problem solving techniques as they mature cognitively.

2. Definitions

Facilitating skills are those thinking operations that are necessary for performing all other thinking operations. Also, they are necessary for mastering basic subject-matter and subject-related skills (mathematical operations, reading, writing, etc.). Both perceptual and organizing skills are fundamental to inferring and predicting. They are necessary and foundational for developing cause and effect relationships. Such skill strategies as inquiry and problem solving and the argument forms of deductive inference and evaluative reasoning can not effectively occur without the use of facilitating skills. These skills are basic to all others.

1. Perceptual Skills. Perception is the ability to receive sensory impressions from the environment and identify and interpret these impressions in relation to past experiences. Thus, perception is not only sensory but involves thought processes as well. To this extent, then, all experience which a child has involves perception, since the way the child will respond to a situation is determined in part by the way which s/he perceives it.

As perceptual information is processed (organized) and becomes a part of the child's conceptual make up, increasingly more abstract imagery and symbolism—such as language—is brought into focus. The development of perceptual skills will serve as a foundation for learning how to organize and classify materials and concepts, as well as for developing language skills appropriate for the expression of these concepts.

Perceiving necessarily involves the concept of **spatial relationships.** The understanding of spaces introduces the child to this concept. The space around the child or an object "in" space are defined in terms of the child's relationship to other parts of the environment—something is "in front of," "behind," "on top of," or "under" some other object or part of the environment. Spatial relationships will include location, mass, width, breadth and size. These relationships will also involve other relations such as color, shape, dimension, measurement and sound (speech, music, rhythms and noise). Perceiving and organizing what is perceived are basic to learning and knowledge.

2. Organizing Skills. The young child depends upon perceptual skills as a means of organizing his or her world. As the child grows older s/he gradually progresses from the use of perceptual (concrete) to conceptual (abstract) categories. During the pre-school and kindergarten years, the child is primarily dependent upon the use of perceptual grouping strategies which include not only grouping by "visible" attributes such as color and shape, but also by other perceptual attributes such as association (relationships) and function (purpose). Older primary children are able to use perceptual groupings (organizing skills) as well as concept categories as they become mentally, as well as sensorily, functional.

2.1. Classification Classification is the grouping of information according to an established pattern. Normally, young children will classify objects and events on the basis of perception and recognition; that is, on observable similarities and differences in properties selected for some preconceived purpose. Classification helps students limit and control data, to place items within a scheme, or to retrieve items from a scheme.

2.2. Sequencing A form of classification, sequencing is the ability to construct an ordered progression of objects or events. Sequencing is essential to understanding the basic concepts of time and number and to reading comprehension. Sequencing is based on the ability to use visual discrimination and, when performed correctly, promotes memory retention.

2.3. Seriation Seriation deals with the ability to place items in order gathered from observation. For example, objects can be arranged in order of increasing or decreasing size or quantity, or in shading from light to dark, or in weight from heavy to light. Again, the understanding of the orderly progression of seriation is especially relevant to the development of concepts related to number. The child not only needs to know the sequence of the numbers but s/he also needs to understand the concept of seriation underlying the fact that six is more than five and less than seven.

QUESTIONING SKILLS

All critical thinking is directed by the feeling that something is wrong and needs to be changed or fixed. Thus, critical thinking is reflective adjustment (assimilation and accommodation) to troubling situations, including confusions in our own thinking. Assuming that critical judgment is an attempt to solve a problem does not mean that a person is always aware of the existence of a problem. A major role of education is problem awareness. It is safe to say, therefore, that critical thinking begins with questioning. R. G. Collingwood reflects (1933): "You can't collect your evidence before you begin thinking...because thinking means asking questions and nothing is evidence except in relation to some definite question." Sometimes students will ask questions which come from stimulation (attention to) by their external environment: a job must be done; a problem must be settled; a technique must be worked out. Certainly externals that cry for solution are often the starting point of critical thinking. The problem situation that originates critical thinking does not necessarily have to be an external situation which disturbs and/or upsets. It may simply be a thought problem which one has proposed to himself or herself. Critical thinking which solves a problem stimulated by external conditions has instrumental or functional value. Critical thinking which focuses on internal problems has intrinsic value. The joy of achievement via orderly reasoning and the satisfaction in neat and precise results are not to be overlooked by teachers.

A. N. Whitehead (1933) reminds us that routine is dominant in any society that is not collapsing. Indeed, the value of habit lies in the organization that it provides. We should also remember that a society of perfect routine would not require intelligence; it would not need to be understood. It would be a society ruled by instinct. Routine tends to

Figure 4.1: Micro-Skill Areas Related to K-3 Organizing Principles

Skill Area: Perceptual Skills (spatial relationships)

	K	Observing, collecting, describing
Grade	1	Comparing, characterizing by resemblance
Levels	2	Exploring, finding new relationships
	3	Looking for inter-relationships

Assumption:

Early learning experiences involve the receiving of sensory information through active exploration and manipulation (creativity skills). As this information is processed, it becomes part of the child's conceptual make up; increasingly more abstract imagery and symbolism, such as language and mathematics, are brought into focus.

Concepts:

People and objects take up space.

The body can be used as a reference point in describing spatial relationships.

There are special words used to describe spatial relationships.

People and objects move through space in orderly ways.

Everything has a shape.

Shapes can be combined or divided to make new shapes.

Names of shapes are used to help describe and identify objects.

Objects can be seriated by size.

Words are sounds used to convey ideas.

Sounds help us identify things we cannot see.

Sounds vary in volume, tempo, pitch and rhythm.

Most people, animals and things make sounds.

produce routine-minded people — people who are so mentally rigid that they cannot easily adjust to change. Also, routine-minded persons find it difficult to take a fresh view of a situation. They attempt to interpret the

Figure 4.1 continued

Skill Area: Classifying Skills		
Grade Levels	K	Listing and matching according to known categories
	1	Sorting by similarities and differences
	2	Understanding and using concepts: those "belonging to" or "not belonging to" a conceptual category
	3	Creating new groupings by combining smaller groups which share a common property and using multiple attributes

Assumption:
Classification of objects and experiences into categories enables the child to organize what s/he is learning about the world. By learning to group things together, the child can reduce the amount of new information which must be remembered.

Concepts:
Objects can be grouped together because they share physical characteristics.
Objects can be grouped together which are commonly associated with each other.
Objects can be grouped together which have similar functions.
Objects can be grouped together which share two or more physical attributes.

new completely in terms of the old. Such people become obsolete quickly; the world, so to speak, passes them by.

Hence, questions have considerable educational value — questions that challenge routine, habit, and old solutions that no longer seem applicable in today's world. Questioning, when contained within an educational setting and connected to critical reflection, is the process which brings about changes in habitual ways of thinking and acting.

Questioning which embodies the problem solving process will stimulate critical thinking as such questions seek solutions and evaluate alter-

Figure 4.1 continued

Skill Area: Seriating Skills		
Grade Levels	K	Ordering according to size, shape and color
	1	Ordering according to volume, pitch and tempo
	2	Ordering according to increasing and decreasing sound, pitch, shade, color; from left to right; and from heavy to its reverse
	3	Ordering according to cause-effect relationships

Assumption:
Seriating implies a kind of order in which there is a regular increase or decrease along a specific dimension. The understanding of the orderly progression of seriation is essential to the development of concepts related to number.

Concepts:
Objects of different size can be arranged in series of increasing or decreasing size.
Colors can be seriated according to the degree of tinting or shading added.
Sounds can be ordered by increasing or decreasing volume, pitch and tempo.
Numbers represent a fixed interval series of increments.

Within the classroom, children will tend to ask questions...

1. when expectations of what will happen do not work out
2. when others do not think as they do,
3. when different lines of thinking lead to contrary conclusions;
4. when someone asks an unexpected questions that interests them but which they cannot handle; and
5. when events are thought to be threatening.

Figure 4.1 continued

Skill Area: Sequencing Skills		
Grade Levels	K	Reproducing objects in a sequence with a model present and from memory
	1	Ordering events in a sequence through action, words, written expression and memory.
	2	Understanding the sequence of natural events, language stories and time.
	3	Ordering according to cause and effect events

Assumption:
   The ability to construct an ordered sequence of objects is one of the child's important means of organizing his or her environment. by condensing information into a familiar sequence, the child can focus his or her most active attention on new, incoming information.

Concepts:
Objects can be arranged in many sequences.
Events can be represented sequentially.
Some sequences are invariable.
Some sequences can be varied to create new effects.
Sequencing is essential for the understanding of time and for reading comprehension.
Sequencing involves the use of visual discrimination; distinctions between right and left; concepts of first, second, and last; and attention to size, shape, and color.

late critical thinking as such questions seek solutions and evaluate alternatives. G. W. Millar (1989) says:

> The ability of students "to put the right question" is a vital skill and permeates the creative problem solving process. Documents from departments of education and indeed, current education literature, emphasize the importance of thinking skills such as questioning. However, their application in classroom practice is lacking.

**Figure 4.2: Categorical Schema of Question Types
Based on the Management of Information Model**

Unsorted Data from
the World

I N F O R M A T I O N

P R O C E S S

Stages in the Management of Information		Question Types
I. Gathering	⟶	Gathering Questions
		Who When
		What Why
		Where How
II. Organizing	⟶	Organizing Questions
		Why
III. Extending	⟶	Extending Questions
		What next...
		What if...

P R O D U C T

L E A R N I N G

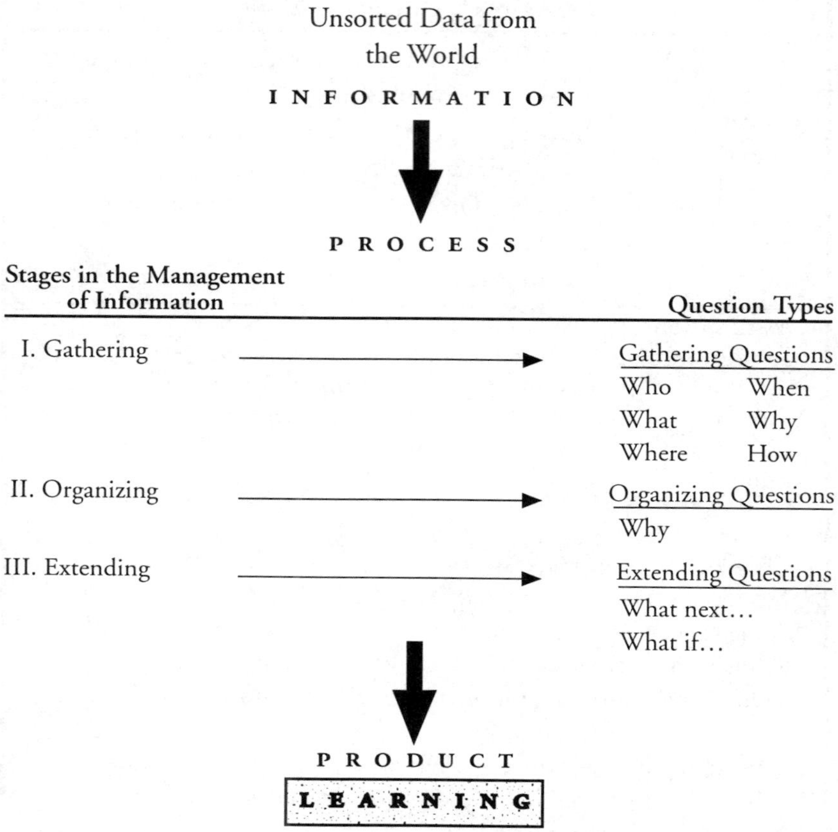

The question types based on the management of information model developed by Himsl and Millar (1989) are particularly useful for teacher and student use. According to Millar, teachers are encouraged to deliberately teach this model to students. He comments: "One of the challenges facing the learner today is how to manage information in a constructive and purposeful way." "The Management of Information Model" is recommended as a productive aid for both students and teachers. This model is divided into three stages for managing information: **gathering information, organizing information** and **extending information.** Each stage is important for understanding, clarifying and creating information. An examination of the model below in Figure 4.2 will demonstrate how certain types of questions can be used to manage information at each stage. Millar says: "The schema is meant to be used as a guideline for students to manage information which ultimately eventuates in effective learning."

Explanation

Stage I: Gathering Information

Factual questions are concerned with basic information. Factual questions occur at all grade levels and are especially common to Grade 3. Factual questions can be answered—perhaps not solely by the information given pictorially or representationaly, but ultimately there is an answer for this type of question. These questions begin with who, what, where, why and how many/much. ("How come" questions do not belong to this category.)

A procedural question seeks information about how something happened. These questions want to know how the event took place or how a specific task was performed. These questions usually begin with "how."

Stage II: Organizing Information

Purposive Questions are divided in two categories: objective and assumptive. This type of question wants to know the reason or the underlying cause of an action. It is a higher-level question; it accepts what is given pictorially but still wants to know why the picture is the way it is. Questions that begin with "how come" are purposive questions.

Purposive assumptive: These questions challenge the initial view; they challenge what is occurring.

Stage III: Extending Information

This type of question accepts the situation given in the picture, but wants to know what happens next. *It projects beyond the apparent* and is considered hypothetical.

A speculative question takes the situation in the picture or event and "moves" the situation farther than what the picture suggests.

This type of question uses the information from the picture, takes an intellectual risk and expands on the information which ultimately creates "new knowledge" about the situation. Often speculative questions begin with "What if" but they can also start with "Is s/he..." or "Are they..." and "I wonder."

ᑲᓇ

Since we have joined critical thinking and problem solving and thought of them as referring to the same basic process, we should also connect questioning more directly to the problem solving model. This has been completed by Bob Swartz (1990) who effectively formulates the basic problem solving or inquiry model of Dewey (1916) in the form of questions. The teacher should understand that the problem solving model, the questioning model provided by Swartz (see Figure 4.3), and the questioning management model developed by Millar and by Himsl and Millar are internally consistent. As we move through the technique of questioning, an effort will be made to join these models in an interconnected whole.

In the Swartz model, section 1 is associated with "gathering information;" sections 2 and 3 are associated with "organizing data" (analyzing ideas and arguments, and assessing the accuracy of ideas); and section 4

Figure 4.3: Bob Swartz: Problem Solving Model Stated in the Form of Questions

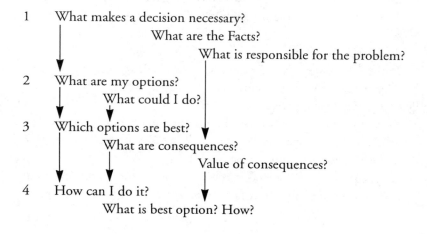

1   What makes a decision necessary?
                         What are the Facts?
                                   What is responsible for the problem?

2   What are my options?
       What could I do?

3   Which options are best?
          What are consequences?
                    Value of consequences?

4   How can I do it?
          What is best option? How?

is associated with extending or applying information. Although there is not a one-to-one correspondence between these two models, there are similarities and both can become useful tools for the teacher.

The pedagogical value of the Swartz model is (1) the statement of the traditional problem solving model in the form of questions, (2) the linkage of these questions to basic micro-thinking skills, themselves stated in the form of questions, and (3) the selection of questions which enable the skill to be infused in to content material, as well as call attention to the essential aspects of the skill itself. Consider the following example:

BASIC THINKING SKILL: COMPARING AND CONTRASTING

The skill of comparing and contrasting falls under the broad skill of clarifying ideas or section 2 of the Swartz model (see Figure 4.3). In the Millar model (see Figure 4.2), the skill of comparing and contrasting is associated with organizing data. A quick reference back to the *Effective Thinking Skills Model, K-3* (page 24), illustrates the fact that comparing and contrasting are skills used at every grade level during the primary years. Thus, we can safely say that comparing and contrasting is a basic thinking operation, critical to the development of formal thinking.

Also, the skill of comparing and contrasting is used when assigning and clarifying the characteristics or attributes of ideas, facts, persons, events, etc. (Figure 4.4) This skill is necessary for more advanced analytical and evaluative thinking and can be understood best by viewing it as one of four cluster skills needed for identifying the significant attributes of a thing, event or idea (of basic information). Therefore, included in the cluster with comparing and contrasting are the associate skills of classifying, sequencing and seriating. Seldom are critical thinking skills used in isolation from other thinking operations. Either micro-thinking skills, such as comparing and contrasting, are used in a larger problem solving format, or they are used in association with similar and supportive critical thinking skill clusters. Examining skills associated with the attribute cluster reveals their logical connections.

Figure 4.4: Attribute Cluster

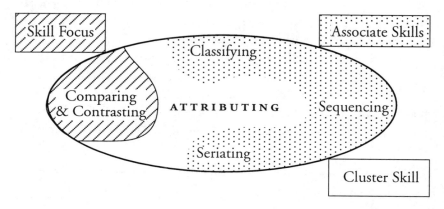

Swartz takes his model a step further by providing a **Teaching Skill Map** (see Figure 4.5) for each mico-skill being taught. We agree with Swartz that these maps greatly help teachers infuse critical thinking into daily lesson plans and regular subject content. An example of the type of teaching maps developed by Swartz is the comparing and contrasting map, stated in the form of questions.

Richard Paul (1989) develops the idea that questioning is basically "wondering aloud about meaning and truth." He reminds teachers that Socratic discussions (based on the skill of questioning) have the function of eliciting and probing student thought; they allow students to develop and evaluate their own thinking; they function to encourage students to

Figure 4.5: Comparing and Contrasting Teaching Skill Map

1. How are they similar?
2. How are they different?
3. What similarities and differences seem significant?
4. What categories or patterns do the significant similarities and differences fall into?
5. What interpretation or conclusion is suggested by the significant similarities and differences?

slow down their thinking and elaborate on it; and they give students the opportunity to develop and test their ideas. *Thus, students are led to synthesize their beliefs into a coherent and well-developed perspective.*

Paul provides the following characteristics of Socratic questioning, characteristics which can be effectively incorporated into the critical thinking/problem solving model emphasized in this book:

1. Teachers are required to take seriously and wonder about what students say and think—what they mean, its significance to them, its relationship to other beliefs, how it can be tested, and to what extent and in what way it is true or makes sense.

2. Socratic questioning is based on the idea that all thinking has a logic or structure and that any one statement or student question only partially reveals the thinking underlying it, expressing no more than a tiny piece of the system of interconnected beliefs of which it is a part. Its purpose is to expose the logic of someone's thought.

3. Socratic questioning assumes that all thinking...
   - has assumptions,
   - makes claims or creates meaning,
   - has implications and consequences,
   - focuses on some things and not others,
   - uses some concepts and not others,
   - is defined by purposes, issues, or problems,
   - uses or explains some facts and not others,
   - is relatively clear, deep, and critical (or their opposites), and
   - is relatively elaborated and multi-logical (or their opposites).

   Critical thinking occurs with an effective, self-monitoring awareness of these points.

4. Socratic instruction can take many forms:
   - questions can come from the teacher or from students,
   - group discussions or one-to-one or with oneself are appropriate, and
   - the instruction can have multi-purposes.

5. Socratic instruction techniques will have in common the belief that the student's thought is developed as a result of the prob-

ing, stimulating questions asked. It requires questioners to "try on" others' beliefs, to imagine what it would be like to accept them and wonder what it would be to believe otherwise.

6. Socratic questioning is structured to take the student's thought from the unclear to the clear, from the unreasoned to the reasoned, from the implicit to the explicit, from the unexamined to the examined, from the inconsistent to the consistent, and from the unarticulated to the articulated.

7. Finally, Socratic questioning requires active listening. The teacher, as well as the student, must look for reasons and evidence, recognize and reflect upon assumptions, discover implications and consequences, seek examples, analogies and objections, and separate what is known from what is believed.

Within young children, cognitive growth occurs through their interactions with the environment and their attempts to construct their own meanings or organize their world. All children can develop the critical thinking skills necessary for successful enculturation if assimilation and accommodation activities are paced appropriately. A tool proven effective for this task is that of artful questioning. Questions placed in the teaching-learning environment, blended with micro- and macro-thinking skills and processes, and carefully sequenced according to developmental stages will greatly improve student learning. Also, these questions should zero in on concept development, the gathering and interpretation of information, the application of generalizations, and the resolution of conflicts (problem solving).

TEACHING STRATEGIES

Cognitive growth can occur in children. We can facilitate cognitive growth by having children manipulate ideas, critically examine them, and try to combine ideas in new and different ways. Productive teaching-for-thinking involves developing strategies which focus on thinking skill infusion and transference. A crucial factor in developing thinking skills and the sequencing of learning experiences is appropriate questioning by the teacher.

Questioning which is open-ended allows for and encourages responses at different levels of abstraction, sophistication and depth, and from different perspectives. Questioning which is developmentally appropriate matches question-pacing with student capacity for mastering the skills at each step. Also, questioning which is appropriately sequenced and consistently and frequently modeled by teachers produces more effective learning outcomes. This is important in that the impact of teaching does not lie only in the frequency of single acts, but also in the ways these questions are combined and integrated into subject content.

Lesson Plan Guide

A lesson plan guide (chapter one, page 16) has been suggested for organizing teaching-for-thinking. The selection of strategies at the primary level will dictate, to one degree or another, the actual methods used in teaching. The lesson plan guide on page 16 should be considered a pre-planning guide. Its role is to help teachers organize ideas, materials, and methods for including critical thinking in subject area content, and blending critical thinking with subject-related facts, concepts, and skills.

Learning objectives. Learning objectives begin with the blending of thinking skills and content in a developmentally appropriate manner (see *Effective Thinking Skills Model,* page 13). Teachers must take care to study the appropriate thinking skills for their grade level (pages 20–26) and then blend these skills at appropriate times in content and content-skill teaching. Major lesson concepts should be taught using the techniques outlined in chapter three of this book.

Student objectives should be written in clear, concise language. These objectives will be shared with students, parents and the principal of the school. Therefore, pre-planning for skill sequence and balance should occur which demonstrates the teacher's knowledge of thinking skills and infusion/transference techniques. Howard and Sandy Black (1990) outline five components of organized thinking that will be useful for planning thinking skill lessons. These include the following:

1. Prepared lessons for infusing thinking skills instruction into content learning.
2. Suggestions for class discussion topics on content lessons and thinking processes.

3. Identification of numerous content objectives for applying thinking skills instruction across the curriculum.
4. Prepared graphics for explaining concepts and guiding classroom discussion.
5. Tools for process writing instruction.

Instructional Practices. There are a wide variety of instructional practices (strategies) available for the teacher. Strategy choices are included in the lesson plan guide that have been proven effective for learning both content and thinking skills. Fogarty and Ballanca (1989) remind us that no matter what philosophy or practice we use for instruction, there are three teachable moments when cognitive processing can enhance a lesson: the set or focus activity, the metacognitive discussion, and the closure.

1. The anticipatory set or advanced organizer *describes the cognitive behavior that occurs in the student's mind when the teacher focuses the student's attention on the lesson's aim. The organizer helps the student go to short term memory to review related material, fit it into the new context and make the needed connections.* Explanations, graphic organizers, pictures and time (patience) are required at the beginning of the lesson to make these connections. This is a valuable teachable moment, especially when teaching-for-thinking.
2. Checking for understanding should occur constantly. *Skill checking will expect that all children take the time to think about their thinking and that the teacher will take the time to elicit sample responses.* The teacher should give special attention to the student's cognitive processing (verbal explanation) of the content, content skill and thinking skill (skill infusion), how the student relates the thinking skill to other skills and in other content areas (skill transference), and the application of the skill to real life situations.
3. Closure. Fogarty and Ballanca remind us that a lesson has three parts, "what," "so what," and "now what," or content, explanation/evaluation, and extension. During content instruction, students give evidence that they understand the critical pieces of

the lesson. They can put the objectives in their own words, and explain and apply the information acquired during the lesson. During the explanation/justification phase, students must make personal applications, link the new learning to past learnings, and lock this newly organized information into larger conceptual contexts and meanings. During extension, the student makes the information come alive as applications are investigated and the new learnings are projected into future situations. *He is encouraged to make abstract ideas practical in a context that he can understand. This brings his thinking into final focus or closure.*

Feedback Correctives are essential for ensuring that students master content and skill objectives. Feedback will come to the teacher in a variety of ways: testing, completing assignments and projects, content and meta-cognitive discussions, oral reading, cooperative learning activities, etc.

Fogarty and Ballanca (1989) provide the following guidelines for teaching-for-thinking and for more completely discovering what students know and how they know it:

1. Avoid "yes" or "no" answers. Keep questions and answers open-ended.
2. All information questions are best followed by questions that call for critical thinking.
3. Ask only one question at a time.
4. Ask extending questions as often as you decide necessary, especially when you are unsure of a student's meaning or if you feel the response could be more specific.
5. Practice wait-time. When using questions to structure meta-cognition, it is important to signal your respect for time to think.
6. Have students write first and then share their responses. Make the classroom climate safe for sharing.
7. Examine your teaching strategy approach. Is it giving you the effects you desire? Read materials on teaching-for-thinking and infuse these techniques into your method.
8. Address thinking skill questions to the entire class. This communicates that all must think about the question.

9. Encourage active listening.
10. Model listening, thinking, logic and the other skills of critical thinking that you are teaching.
11. Acknowledge skillful thinking.
12. Encourage students to answer each other. Tell them that you will be responsible to be where you can hear, but that they should talk to the class.
13. Encourage cooperative learning by helping others think and by paying attention when another student is speaking.
14. When you hear a student using appropriate thinking skills, acknowledge that. When they need refinement, suggest changes.
15. It helps students if major lesson concepts are processed in each lesson. This will increase metacognitive readiness.
16. Feedback correctives which focus on critical thinking should look for and acknowledge improved intellectual behavior that can be reinforced & extended. Positive feedback should be a daily teaching practice. Re-teach when necessary. Enrich and extend those concepts and skills that are successfully learned.

How do we distinguish between critical and non-critical thinking? This is an important question for the classroom because teachers and students must be able to identify the quality of ideas expressed in discussion and arguments. To know critical thinking when we hear and see it is sometimes difficult. For this reason, we have provided the *Effective Thinking Skills Model. ETSM* is a continuum of thinking skills that will identify and perhaps judge the degree of critical thinking that occurs in classroom discussions. Thinking critically may be thought of as a movement from the lower to the higher levels of cognitive and affective concerns, from preoperations to abstract thought. *Criticalness* includes significant growth in awareness and sensitivity to problems. It challenges as well as deepens our understanding of alternatives available to solve a given problem or resolve a particular issue. It could be argued that movement from an effort to understand and derive meaning through critical thinking and well-grounded judgments is one way of viewing the continuum of thought in an educational and cognitive (or philosophic) sense.

Thinking Aloud

Young thinkers at the primary level should be encouraged to accurately observe and critically inquire about the world in which they live. They need to be encouraged to express and clarify their thoughts through classroom interactions. The ideas generated by these experiences can be extended through reading and writing projects. Also, activities such as role-playing, puppetry, and creative art can be included in problem solving exercises.

A useful strategy for teaching-for-thinking that requires explanation is correctly called **thinking aloud**. Over forty years ago, Bloom and Broder (1950) found that a major barrier to understanding and teaching problem solving is that *thinking* is generally done inside a person's head where it is hidden from view. The teacher has difficulty teaching thinking because thinking is unseen, and the learner has difficulty in learning how to think from a teacher because the process of modeling thinking is also unseen. The teacher is unable to observe the beginner's practicing. They also have difficulty pointing out flaws and demonstrating to the student how to improve. Likewise, the beginner cannot observe how the teacher thinks or solves problems.

One way around this barrier is to have students *think aloud* while they solve problems. Also, teachers can model thinking to students by giving careful instructions, using proper questioning techniques, or orally and graphically modeling the thinking skill or problem solving process. When Bloom and Broder had students think aloud as they solved problems, a striking difference was observed between those who were academically successful and those who were not. Unsuccessful students were mentally careless and superficial in solving problems. They rushed through problems, failing to comprehend what was needed to select correct answers. When encouraged to reread the problem, and take care in comprehending the problem, they often understood it better and proceeded correctly. Even then, however, they were not thorough and settled for a rough interpretation. Unsuccessful students also tended to be passive in their thinking. They spent little time considering a question and hurried to choose an answer based on a few clues, such as a feeling, impression or guess.

By contrast, successful students made a purposeful and active attack on problems. When a question was unclear, they employed a lengthy sequential analysis for arriving at an answer. They began with what was understood, drew on other pertinent information that was in their cognitive-memory, and used a chain of steps that brought them to a solution.

In order to assist students with their critical thinking skills, Whimbey

Successful Problem Solver	Unsuccessful Problem Solver
1. Planned, sequential activities	1. Careless
2. Active rather than passive	2. Superficial
3. Utilization of cognitive memory	3. Hurries through problems
	4. Weak comprehension skills
4. Persistence, using a step-by-step method to find a solution	5. Settles for rough interpretation
	6. Passive
	7. Impatient

and Lochhead (1982) have developed a workbook that includes *thinking aloud* responses of successful students and professionals. Their research illustrates two major characteristics that distinguish successful from unsuccessful students: (1) the step-by-step approach and (2) carefulness. These two characteristics illustrate student cognitive ability, experiences and task-persistence. Successful students have a concern for quick retracking when ideas become confusing, and for rechecking, reviewing and recording information to be sure that errors have not crept into their work and nothing has been overlooked.

Only in recent years have educators suggested that children be taught to think and solve problems in a systematic way as they are taught other academic skills. During the primary years, we appreciate and encourage creativity and spontaneity in action and speech. We certainly care that young students are given the opportunity for a free, open and quick response to their environment and their own feelings. Room must be made for the building of a creative, supportive and happy learning environment. Although we take care to maintain this data-driven, inductive and free response to the environment, the socialization process demands more cognitive control, deliberation, caution, thoughtfulness and planning prior to actions and speech. The balance of creative expression and intelligent deliberation do not have to be countervariants in the educational process. Careful attention to creativity research reveals many ways in which cognition and creativity can be joined for maximum results. The Future Problem Solving Program (Crabbe 1989) is a case in point. Anne Crabbe says that in this program, students "learn that there is more than one option open to them in almost every situation and that the selection of the best option is up to them. They also learn that if they do not make the choices that will govern their lives, someone else will. With the skills and knowledge gained from participation in Future Problem Solving, students are far better equipped to take control of their personal futures."

Camp and Bash (1981) have also created a "think aloud" program for youngsters that helps them think more effectively and behave more thoughtfully. Although originally designed as a theraputic program for aggressive boys, this program can easily be modified as a cognitive skills or problem solving program that can be used with any child who responds without adequately thinking through the consequences of actions.

Think Aloud begins with the premise that *verbal mediation is the use of language as an internal regulator and tool of rational thought and logic.* We may describe this approach as talking to ourselves in order to guide problem solving. Verbal mediation is a striking feature of the shift in thinking that occurs in children between the ages of five and seven years. Milner (1967) describes this shift as from the "mammalian" principle to the "human" principle in thought. White (1965) describes this shift as that which occurs from the "associative processing" to the "cognitive processing" of information. Prior to the age of five, youngsters use language primarily as a social and instrumental tool. They tend to respond to events superficially, reacting to surface clues, generalizing on the basis of perceptual similarities, and reasoning in an associative fashion. After this time they are capable of inhibiting impulsive reactions through internal linguistic controls, responding to conceptually meaningful relationships, and of substituting logic and reasoning for associations. Camp and Bash conclude that the development of verbal mediation ability is associated with the:

1. internalization of the inhibitory function of language which serves to block impulsive and associative responding in both cognitive and social situations; and
2. utilization of linguistic tools in learning, problem solving and forethought.

If the capacity for verbal mediation responses is deficient, critical judgment will be retarded. Deficient verbal mediated responses are found in retarded and brain damaged children, and in those who are developmentally delayed (by limited experiences). Those limited by experience or socialization (the lack of human contact) will fail to use conceptual and critical thinking skills in appropriate situations or will fail to control nonverbal behavior. In either case, the failure to utilize critical judgment because of verbal mediation deficits will cause educational problems. The information provided by Camp and Bash consistently links verbal mediation to cognitive function. Thus, we are able to conclude that verbal mediation is a requisite skill to successful problem solving, decision making, and critical judgments.

Cognitive modeling is an important teaching process for young children. It involves the teacher in thinking aloud activities. Cognitive modeling is the teacher's overt verbalization of his or her own self-guiding thought processes or self-instructional activity and represents a major departure from traditional educational approaches. In the modeling of the problem solving or critical thinking skill activity, the teacher usually points out what the children should do each step of the way. For new skills and concepts, this may be necessary. Also, when a new skill is being applied to a new situation or when a learned skill is being transferred from one subject area (or context) to another, the verbalization of thought processes will be valuable (Hetherington and McIntyre 1975).

Cognitive modeling has a facilitating effect on the acquisition of new cognitive skills. Research shows that cognitive modeling also assists with the development of verbal mediation skills and the development of internal control sought for aggressive children. Rappaport and Rappaport

(1975) suggest that improved self-esteem might better a child's achievement, itself a side effect of developed verbal mediation and problem solving skills. Thinking aloud and using problem solving, decision making, and cognitive modeling techniques will provide youngsters a good chance of performing successfully in our schools, raising their self-esteem, and reinforcing their positive behaviors.

CHAPTER FIVE
Processing Skills (Grades 4–6)

❦

THE ELEMENTARY STUDENT
Concrete Operations

We find that the basic purpose of education is to produce rational human beings who can be confronted with an unfamiliar situation, gather information about it, make a decision on the basis of that information, and demonstrate that decision through various human behaviors. That is what schools are for. This implies that teaching practices should focus on understanding those concepts necessary for cultural survival, help students generate consistent judgments based on these concepts, and assist them as they infer from these concepts and judgments behavioral habits that entail moral and productive living. This idea is supported by both Dewey (1929) and Bruner (1966) who maintain that the experience we have in doing something is what teaches us. Learning is not represented by the information (something mistakenly called "knowledge") which the learner accumulates during the experience. Neither is learning represented by becoming acquainted with "something" after it has been accomplished. Rather, as Bruner comments:

> We teach a subject not to produce little living libraries on that subject, but rather to get a student to think mathematically for himself, to consider matters as the historian does, to take part in the process of knowledge-getting. Knowing is process not a product.

Are we educating our children for the wrong future? A primary function of the elementary school is to provide learners with the intellectual tools, discipline, and framework necessary to understand the new problems we face. Education, in other words, is not preparation for life; it is life. Because of this belief, elementary schools are obligated to reproduce within the classroom the typical conditions of social life. In 1961, the Educational Policies Commission said that schools must provide the conditions under which each individual can develop freedom of mind. If a mind is free, it is able to apply certain definite rational processes to the solution of problems and making of decisions. These processes include **recalling and imagining, classifying and generalizing, comparing and evaluating, analyzing and synthesizing,** and **deducing and inferring.** In other words, the general purpose of education is to develop the fundamental mental processes that constitute thinking.

In this chapter our purpose is to focus on the elementary student. Teaching-for-thinking implies that we will help this student develop concepts, make judgments, and, infer from these, meaningful behaviors. Elementary students in grades four through six are moving from the early stages of concrete thinking (perhaps the later stages of preoperational thinking) into the stage of concrete operations. This movement is gradual and does not take place all at once. At the concrete operational stage, the elementary learner is at the door of logical thinking but is not yet ready, cognitively, to enter that door. This child is able to take ideas about things, events, persons and places from an investigation, rearrange them mentally, experiment with them, and make statements about what s/he believes. The concrete thinker is able to think about h/her beliefs and assumptions and, in turn, think about h/her own thinking. During this stage, says Piaget, children operate on objects (concrete sensory experiences) but not yet on verbally expressed hypotheses.

At the elementary level, elementary students will be frustrated unless they have the actual objects, events, situations and problems to work on. Although skill acquisition begins with verbal learning, to become autonomous thinkers, children must practice their thinking by applying it to actual, concrete situations and problems. The concrete stage of intellectual development begins somewhere between six and one half and seven and one half years and continues, according to Piaget, until ages eleven or twelve. Recent research suggests that this age range might even be extended (Arlin 1987). Arlin's test results show that approximately two-thirds of sixth through ninth graders are at the concrete level of thinking, 14.5 percent are in transition, and 25 percent are at the level of formal reasoning. Clearly then, the upper age limit on concrete operations is much higher for some students than for others.

The curricular implications of this growing body of research is clear. For some students at the middle, high school and college levels, cognitive growth has been uneven or has not matured with mental capability. For this reason, we shall discuss the concept of "thinking in transition" with reference to the middle and high school student in the next chapter. These students, like the elementary student, must first master the critical thinking skills of concrete operations before moving into the level of formal thinking. The bulk of elementary student's education should consist of direct, experiential kinds of learning—learning that allows the student to interact with objects, ideas, situations and problems across several disciplines. This type of learning is called "inquiry" and inquiry leads to the development of cognitive powers.

The concrete operational thinker will focus on the actual data of experience—situations, concrete objects and issues. They will organize this data and perform mental experiments leading to understanding and accommodating behaviors. The skills learned and practiced during the primary years—perceiving, classifying, sequencing, seriating, comparing and contrasting, and searching for causal explanations—are the cognitive foundation of concrete operations. At the high concrete, transitional and early formal levels of thinking, the student will begin to explore the consequences and implications of h/her thinking. During the early years of concrete operations, consequences and implications will be discussed but not fully developed or understood. The basic difference between the concrete and formal stages of cognitive development is that at the formal operational stage the learner can reason from ideas and does not depend on objects as s/he does in the concrete operational stage.

In this chapter we will focus on inquiry as a teaching method that is consistent with and supportive of concrete operational thinking. It is a requisite and logical practice supportive of problem solving which requires the use of both concrete and formal operations. Inquiry is a necessary educational practice because it provides the opportunity for the learner to understand concepts and develop appropriate meanings and behaviors. When understanding and meaning are missing, the student is in a stage of disequilibrium. Inquiry is, then, a methodology of equilibrium. John R. Anderson (1983) calls this process **procedural learning**. He says that the one term most central to procedural learning is **production**. Anderson comments:

> Productions provide the connection between declarative knowledge and behavior....The productions constitute the procedural knowledge...that is, knowledge about how to do things....Procedural learning occurs only in executing a skill; one learns by doing. This is one of the reasons why procedural learning is a much more gradual process than declarative learning....When an existing set of productions uses declarative knowledge to guide new behavior, it is said to be applying the knowledge interpretively. In certain senses the production set is using this knowledge the way a computer interpreter uses the statements in a program. After the knowledge has been applied interpretively a number of times, a set of productions can be compiled that applies the knowledge directly.

According to Anderson, there are three basic stages of skill acquisition or **production** development (see Figure 5.1, page 113):

1. During the **interpretive stage** skill productions use declarative (verbal) representations relevant to the skill to guide behavior. Here the teacher tells, instructs, demonstrates and models the skill. Verbal instruction connects related student memories, providing for conceptual organization, meaning and understanding.

2. Once meaning is provided, **skill-specific productions** are compiled. It is during stage two that the skill performance is "smoothed out." Errors in the initial understanding of the skill are gradually detected and eliminated. Stage one can be correctly called the stage of "verbal rehearsal" for there the learner uses declarative information, held in working memory, relevant to the skill. At the second stage, the steps and procedures are being created for the skill. This is called the **associative stage**.

3. The **autonomous stage** consists of the gradual and continued improvement of the skill. The teacher should now use strength-

ening processes to speed up the rate of skill application and tuning processes to account for the nuances of skill applications (when, where, how). Strengthening processes use examples of successful or unsuccessful skill application to teach how to use the skill. Anderson recommends practice to improve skill expertise. One should compare Anderson's insights with those of Thorndike (1932; 1935) whose research occurred fifty years earlier. Tuning mechanisms will focus on skills correlation, the integration of skills with subject matter, and nuances of skill application from one context to another.

Anderson summarizes his comments on inquiry and skill development by saying that "to function successfully, these learning mechanisms require goal structures and planning structures. As skills develop they are compiled and better tuned...."

The Inquiry Classroom

In her book *Overcoming Math Anxiety* (1980), Sheila Tobias says, "We are becoming a society where test-taking skills are the prerequisite for a chance at getting a good education, and where hard work, hope, and ambition are in danger of becoming nothing more than meaningless concepts." We should reconsider as we continue the quantification and mechanization of teaching and learning: (1) what is meant by a "good education" and (2) "why" all students should receive a "good education."

Perhaps we should address these two questions separately. In the first place, "a good education" is one that does not limit students but prepares

---

Although this book focuses on the development of thinking skills, this in no way is meant to suggest that such skills are an end unto themselves. Thinking skills are simply the cognitive skills (the means) required to achieve a more satisfying life in our contemporary world. When taught without meaning and purpose, thinking skills become lifeless and are thought of as having no value other than those values associated with schooling. We cannot let this happen.

Figure 5.1: Stages of Skill Acqusition

Example: Causal Explanation

Searching for a reliable indicator of "why" a belief is held involving describing, explaining, predicting and choosing: searching for the relationship between cause and effect.

1. The Interpretive Stage

Taught by declarative representations, verbal directives, and verbal characterization

1. *Propositions—Teacher.* "Can you tell me why some people are leaders and others are not leaders?"

2. *Related strings of sequential information*—"Can you summarize some of the main characteristics of 'leadership'?"

3. *Spatial pictures*—"Here are two pictures of persons that have been called 'leaders.' Do you know or can you find out why they are called 'leaders?'"

Students verbally rehearse the information required to execute the skill using new knowledge and experience to provide meaning.

2. The Associative Stage

The associative stage functions to smooth out the skill. The purpose of this stage is the detection and elimination of errors.

The teaching objective is the production of skill-specific responses. Here, skills are applied through continued research and previous knowledge. Each step is associated with the next step and the whole process is then evaluated.

Students will discover **why** certain persons are called "leaders" and will clarify the concept of **leadership**.

3. The Autonomous Stage

Important for remediation and enrichment

The autonomous stage is the stage of skill improvement and utilizes:

A. **Strengthening processes** made up of examples of success and failure (in this case, leaders and non-leaders). The skill focus will be on discriminating among those examples that work and those that don't work.

B. **Tuning processes** focus on correlations between skill combinations and integrated subjefct matter (applying causal explanation to a variety of subjects and "leadership" in a variety of ways).

Generalization: Students will summarize the concept of "leadership" and will generalize the reasons why some people become leaders and others do not.

and opens them to a future of growth and employment possibilities. An education that is limiting will also limit these same students to lives of menial employment. By placing emphasis on a future of growth we are at once putting our faith in hard work, hope and ambition.

All students should be given the opportunity to participate in "a good education." As Tobias asks, "At a time when our economy requires better educated workers than ever before, can we afford to let abstract measures of ability curtail the educational aspirations and potential accomplishments of our children?" I have long been an advocate of differentiated education for students with high academic potential. The production of the Philosophy for Young Thinkers series is a testimony to my effort to provide an "appropriate" curriculum which meets the academic needs of these youngsters. On the other hand, we should never reserve critical and creative thinking for only those students. All children can and should be taught to think. Thinking is not the sole province of gifted students or gifted programs.

Research says that grouping students on the basis of intellect and ability often dooms the so-called non-gifted to academic failure and watered-down classes. Low-track placement can also erode students' self esteem, resulting in a "sense of inadequacy." If critical thinking and creative teaching are used with only the academically gifted student, we are missing the opportunity to engage the intellect of all students and move them through concrete operational thinking into formal thought processing. We now know that teaching all students to reason with content-related materials and about life situations not only increases test scores, but also prepares and motivates them for a lifetime of productivity and success. What we have learned in gifted education needs to be implemented in all classrooms for all students. Gifted education and gifted educators must today become part of the solution to educational reform and not part of the problem.

Consider the established sequence in Figure 5.2. The question is how can we move from 1 and 2 to the goals embodied in 3 and 4? We can achieve these goals in the following way:

1. Concentrate on positive values: self-reliance, participatory learning, authenticity, and intellectual self-esteem.
2. Refocus our educational motives by getting rid of our fear of

novelty and diversity and replacing it with curiosity, a passion for precision and the desire to share.

3. Restructure our teaching by replacing teaching that is expert-dominated with one that is discovery-oriented. We must move away from teaching that is a structured monologue and provide opportunities for students to interpret their experiences and opportunities that reward reflective intelligence in all of its forms and stages. Learners can develop the ability to interpret their own experiences or they can remain enslaved to the interpretations of others.

Figure 5.2: Student Vulnerability

Student vulnerability is linked to

either   1. knowledge and skill inequality,
        2. which in turn leads to teacher-dependency,

or   3. independence, self-esteem, and self-identity, and
     4. academic success and social mobility.

Teaching thinking to all students means that we will engender in learners the capacity to accept responsibility for their own development within the social group while noting that one's self development must take place in the context of a general respect for the interests of others in the group. This attitude will decrease student and teacher vulnerability as truth-fostering motives permeate the learning environment. E. A. Burtt (1965) reflects:

> The pursuit of sound knowledge in any field rests on the sustaining energy these motives provide. As they achieve their own natural unity under growing awareness, perhaps they constitute the general motive that would be called "truthfulness"—the aspiration for cognitive integrity.

Without developed thinking abilities, our students may remain imprisoned in the prejudices derived from common sense experiences and in the grip of the arrogant dogmatism of those who have never traveled into the region of liberating doubt. We should be reminded that doubt serves as the necessary condition for open-mindness, not neutrality. It will also teach us to tolerate differences of opinion, for we can hardly claim to be willing to revise our own views in the light of objections which others may introduce if we are not tolerant and open-minded. There is no room for dogmatism in the learning environment.

THE SKILLS OF INQUIRY

John A. McCollum (1978) reminds us:

> the necessity of developing the skill of self-generative learning in each learner grows more obvious and urgent every day. The incredible and accelerating explosion of knowledge, coupled with the frighten-ingly complex social, political, and economic problems of our con-temporary era, demands an educational process that produces active, autonomous, self-generative learners. Productive individuals in the contemporary world must have the emotional stability to confront continuous change and the necessary skills to engage in a continuous process of personal problem solving.

McCollum observes that the educational process found in many class-rooms "does not contribute significantly to the development of this type of individual....The predominant educational process in many class-rooms encourages learners to avoid the responsibility of their own ideas—to distrust or ignore their own capacity for finding, creating, and testing meaning in the world."

One way of overcoming this problem is by turning our classrooms in-to places of **inquiry** involving critical thinking processes and such meth-ods as diagnosis, speculation and hypothesis testing. The method of in-quiry gives students the opportunity to confront problems and generate and test ideas for themselves. In general, the concept of inquiry is based on the assumption that the teacher's role is one of creating an environ-ment which encourages students to generate and test their own under-standings and meanings. The emphasis is on ways of examining and ex-plaining information (events, facts, situations, behaviors, etc.). Students, when taught for the purposes embodied in inquiry, are encouraged to evaluate the usefulness of their beliefs and ideas by applying them to new problem situations and inferring from them implications for future courses of action.

Robert Glasser (1966) finds two processes associated with inquiry or discovery learning of importance to critical thinking. The first, inductive processes, are teacher-guided and structured. The student's responsibility is to generate solutions to teacher-created problems and test them through experimentation and application. The second, trial and error, is a relatively unguided sequence to which learners apply their own structure. J. Richard Suchman (1962) agrees that students should gather their own information, raise and test hypotheses, build theories, and test them empirically. He finds basic intuitive processes in the learner that are often negated by classroom management and structure. Suchman points out that inquiry controlled by the learner, and the teacher must provide the conditions by which inquiry occurs. The teacher's role is (1) to engineer conceptual reorganization in each child, and (2) to bring about the child's accommodation to discrepant events. This occurs by planning a series of discovery experiences, drawing on past memories, and focusing attention on selected aspects of the environment.

According to Glasser, Suchman and McCollum, these fundamental steps characterize the discovery method from which we are able to generate the basic processes needed for inquiry. From these processes, we are able to summarize the critical thinking skills that call for instruction and clarification. From their collective points of view, inquiry is the scientific process by which knowledge is generated and validated. To successfully implement this process, the teacher must remain sensitive to the meanings that students bring to school. On the teacher's part, there must be a maximum of "tuning in" to the personal meanings, concepts and understandings that students reveal.

To improve classroom discussions leading to inquiry/discovery learning, S. I. Hayakawa (1979) claims that teachers must pay particular attention to the words that students "use. These include the following:

1. **Report Words.** These are declarative statements that describe what a person has seen, heard or felt. Report words are based on observation or measurement and are therefore verifiable.

Example: The student reports: "The car ran off the road."
Justification: "I saw the car run off the road."

2. **Inferences.** These are statements about the unknown made on the basis of the known. In each case, the statement *infers* a situation that may or may not be so. Inferences have meaning when clarified and verified in report language.

   The student says: "The car ran off the road because the driver was drunk."
   Justification: "The policeman gave the driver a sobriety test and verified that the driver was intoxicated."

3. **Judgments.** These are statements that express approval or disapproval of occurrences, persons or objects, or alternative solutions to a problem. The judgment becomes meaningful when a basis for the judgment is given in report language.
   Example: The student says: "I think it is bad to drink and drive."
   Justification: "Many people have died because of drunk drivers."

The language used by students during inquiry can be summarized into strategies for instructional purposes. It is the responsibility of the teacher to design and conduct inquiry discussions that enable students to generate and test their own ideas of what is "true" or "right" or "good." Important to remember (McCollum 1978) is that inquiry will begin with **specific data**, call for **concept clarification**, and, from these, students will be able to create **generalizations**. Generalizations must then be explained and verified. From these verifications, theories and inferences will be made.

This process will involve the following skills:

1. **Describing** (using observation, memory, and recall). A describing question calls for a verifiable observation to be given in report language. It will be common for the response to be given in the form of an inference or a judgment. Reports, inferences and judgments must then be separated for further clarification.

2. **Explaining** (using interpretation and convergent thinking). Explaining is language that either asks for or gives the solution to a

puzzling phenomenon or discrepancy. It seeks the relationship between cause and effect—looks for a specific cause to explain an existing effect.

3. **Predicting** (using extrapolation and divergent thinking). Predicting either asks for or gives the future consequences of an action, event or situation. It is speculation about what might happen in the future.

4. **Choosing** (valuing or evaluating). Choosing either asks for or gives a choice between two or more alternatives. It involves analyzing alternatives and formulating judgments as to which is better, best, worse, good, or bad (that is, which solution best solves the existing dilemma).

In Figure 5.3, these processes are related to the thinking skills defini-

---

Children enter school as fundamentally non-culpable, uncritical and self-serving thinkers. The educational task is to help them to become, as soon as possible and as fully as possible, responsible, fairminded, critical thinkers, empowered by intellectual skills and rational passions.

Richard Paul, (1989)

---

tive of the inquiry process contained in Figure 1.3, the *Effective Thinking Skills Model 4–6* (page 25). From this chart is generated specific critical thinking skill clusters that demonstrate the interrelation of the intellectual skills that should be infused into the elementary curriculum—in every subject—and practiced by students.

Figure 5.4 (page 121) has been provided for explicating the thinking skill clusters in Figure 5.3. It is important that we understand (1) the relationship of major cluster skills in order to maintain skill clarity and proficiency, and (2) the relationship of cluster skills and subskills to student cognitive development. By focusing on skill clusters, we will be able to apply critical thinking in a variety of ways, infuse them into the cur-

Major Processes	Grade 4	Grade 5	Grade 6
	GRADE LEVEL SKILLS		
Describing	Using multiple descriptors	Comparing and contrasting	(extension of grades 4–5)
Explaining	Explaining cause and effect relationships	Identifying and classifying asumptions	Using analogy and metaphor in interpretations and explanations
Predicting	Formulating simple hypotheses and testing for reliability Analyzing relevant and irrelevant data	Modifying hypotheses	Testing and evaluating hypotheses
Choosing	Finding conclusions Making inferences	Evaluating alternatives	Generalizing and transferring concepts

Figure 5.3: The Skills of Inquiry

riculum, and provide a means by which students are able to broaden their understanding of the diversity of skill vocabulary.

Each associative skill in a skill cluster represents certain nuances and/or purposes (ways of using) of the skill. There is also a "spin off" effect related to skill instruction. That is, a particular associative skill can be developed and extended throughout a lesson for a particular purpose; the student may require a fuller interpretation and explanation of the skill or the teacher may wish to take the skill to a more refined level.

USING THE INQUIRY METHOD

John Dewey

The exploration-invention-discovery mode of instruction represents inquiry, and the inquiry method is essentially incomplete if any one of

Figure 5.4: Skill Clusters

ATTRIBUTING

Purpose: Describe the characteristics of people, places, things, events, ideas, etc.

Related Skills:
Comparing/contrasting
Classifying
Sequencing
Seriating

Major skill extension:
Comparing and Contrasting
Clarifying ideas
Significant similarities and
  differences
Significant patterns and concepts
Interpreting significant similar-
  ities and differences

INFERRING

Purpose: Make statements about the unknown on the basis of the known

Related Skills:
Hypothesizing
Predicting
Generalizing (drawing conclusions)
Analyzing relevant/irrelevant data

Major skill extension:
Analyzing
Analyzing for bias
Evaluating assumptions
Checking for consistency
Searching for casual explanation

CAUSAL EXPLANATION

Purpose: Assess how well new data fits what else we know.

Related Skills:
Searching for causes
Accounting for or against the likeli-
  hood of a conclusion
Assessing relevant evidence
Explaining relationships

Major skill extension:
Explaining
Connecting bits and pieces of
information
Gaining overall picture of how
things work
Ranking rival conclusions in order
of plausibility
Judging relevance of new
information

EVALUATING

Purpose: Express approval or disapproval for alternative solutions.

Related Skills:
Prioritizing
Assessing reliability of evidence
Establishing criteria of valuation
Generalizing
Making decisions

Major skill extension:
Generalizing
Formulating simple hypotheses
Stating of observation reports
Testing observation reports to
  determine if they confirm or fal-
  sify the generalization

these modes is missing. Some have labeled inquiry the "discovery" method of learning, but discovery is only one segment of a total inquiry program. Discovery can and does go on during exploration and it does not reach its zenith until **conceptual invention** has occurred. Inquiry, therefore, is really an attitude which is established in the classroom by the teacher during daily interactions with learners.

Inquiry will not always result in finding a solution to a problem. The value of using the inquiry method is the search for knowledge and understanding. It is during the *search* that the thinking ability of the student is being challenged and developed.

Perhaps it was John Dewey who stressed the importance of inquiry more than any other American educator. Alfred North Whitehead commented that Dewey cast doubt on the purposes of conventional education (information transmission) and stressed instead the method of inquiry as the teaching method that can lead to the development of rational powers.

While at the University of Chicago, Dewey began experimenting with new ideas of progressive education and put them to work in a laboratory school that was based on the premise that education is a social process. Accordingly, the most important human capacity—intelligence—was emphasized. Moreover, by elevating intelligence, reason and teaching were joined with the real processes going on in the world. For Dewey, human intelligence operated in the material world as an instrument of change, thus having strong political and social implications.

Dewey's purpose was to discover how thought functions in the experimental determination of future consequences. His goal was to establish universally recognized distinctions by drawing them from the **reconstruction** or **mediation** functions ascribed to reason. We must continue to emphasize the concepts of reconstruction and mediation with reference to intelligence. Dewey says that thought does not get started and the intelligence is not engaged until a person is involved in a problematic situation. A person must be "up against it," in a situation of genuine perplexity, confusion and uncertainty, for inquiry to begin. Fundamentally, the puzzlement initiates (1) a survey of what the situation is—ascertaining of data and identifying the problem; (2) a separating or classifying of those elements that remain stable and unproblematic from those that are the source of the difficulty; (3) a leap toward hypothesis, an imaginative reconstruction of the situation such that the elements now blocking further smooth functioning of the person's life will be rearranged and fitted into the stable elements (according to Dewey, this is the essential contribution of intelligence—what Piaget calls "accommodation"); and (4) the hypothesis is put to use and, if effective, it leads to the completion of the initial tendency of the person, and the problematic situation disappears (1910; 1916; 1929).

For Dewey, reflection has its home in practical situations and is explicitly adaptive in concept and function. The function of intelligence is not that of copying objects in the environment (memorization), but rather "a taking account of the ways in which more effective and more profitable relations with these objects may be established in the future." Propositions then are a means of reconstructing and transforming the world around us, of carrying the situation to conclusion. Thus, when a person judges that s/he should become a teacher, s/he creates conditions which make possible the satisfactory completion of that situation.

Dewey emphasizes the **mediating** role of intelligence. By using one's intelligence, a person recognizes his or her increased liberation and intelligent control of the course of events which are achieved through accurate discovery. The idea of completeness, for Dewey, is a relative matter, depending on the ends pursued. Given certain ends, certain means will be appropriate, and it is the task of intelligence to put the ends and means in proper relation to each other. It is never a matter of taking all possibilities into account but only a matter of relative adequacy. A correct assessment of the situation leading to its satisfactory completion justifies our calling a judgment which leads up to it, a "true" judgment. It remains a mere hypothesis until it results in action. The issue is the truth or falsity of the judgment.

This issue is brought forth by Dewey in his unwillingness to ascribe cognitive significance to a mere contemplation of a perception. Perceptions are only materials for propositions and judgments; they have no cognitive status in themselves. They may be, of course, conclusions from other data previously experienced, but, in either case, **inference** is necessary for judgment to take place. Thus, the exercise of intelligence involves a transaction, a movement from data to conclusions. Here we have what Dewey calls the **means-ends continuum**, whereby means can conceivably become ends in themselves, and ends, in turn, function as means toward further ends.

For Dewey, life is much more varied and creative than what Darwin demonstrated, especially when it is guided by liberated intelligence. This was the view of Kant a century before as he saw in the categories of the mind (intuition, understanding and reason) a way to bring common sense into the light of truth. Truth is public and will more likely be attained if inquiry proceeds on a broad, educational front. A scientific approach (inquiry) calls for collaboration and discussion, a democratically conceived community effort. The insights of Dewey in the first half of this century provide for us a point of departure for our emphasis on processing skills (skills of reconstruction and mediation). Through inquiry students are permitted to "find out" for themselves and utilize their growing intelligence in an active, interactive, learning process.

Classroom Inquiry

When is inquiry functioning? According to Azbell (1977), inquiry is taking place when:

1. students are treated as investigators;
2. a problem, situation or topic to explore surfaces in the classroom setting;
3. students are encouraged to investigate this problem and generate solutions and answers that are relevant to it;
4. the inductive method of discovery is being used by students; and
5. the information or evidence is new to students and requires their interpretation.

When using the inquiry method with students, the teacher should carefully consider the observations (Casey 1979) in Figure 5.5 and 5.6.

The inquiry approach to learning requires that the learner find solutions to problems rather than being told or indoctrinated toward one specific, prechosen answer. The learner is provided background on the steps of problem solving and solution finding, and given instruction in the critical thinking skills required by the inquiry process. Students are

Figure 5.5: Characteristics of Inquiry Teaching

Most inquiry units will not provide all the information necessary to solve a problem. Rather, the inquiry approach generally follows certain steps or logical patterns to reach a conclusion.

The teacher should also understand that when using inquiry, it is important for the students to internalize factual information. This information will become the foundation for future research and investigations.

In an inquiry lesson, the scope of the study will tend to feed off itself and become larger. As the investigation moves toward conclusion, selection and relativity are important processes in judging the importance of information and the selection of alternatives.

Finally, in inquiry the role of the teacher will move back and forth from planning to facilitating the learning process, rather than telling and testing what factual and conceptual information that has been learned. The teaching/learning signals in the inquiry classroom will not always come from the teacher in a continuous onstage model as a presenter of information. Instead students will be confronted with the responsibility of explaining information, not just listening to the teacher's explanation of the material under investigation.

Figure 5.6: Steps of Inquiry Implementation

Step One: The problem to be solved is stated clearly and accurately by students and by the teacher. Simplicity should be the guide in making the problem statement.

Step Two: After a preliminary study and discussion of the problem, proposition or troubling information, the students should be encouraged to construct a tentative answer to it called a "hypothesis."

Step Three: A full investigation should be launched in which the hypothesis is tested, evaluated and redefined with reference to new information.

Step Four: Students should formulate a final conclusion or solution to the problem.

Step Five: The entire process should be reviewed with a "learning team" who serve as a sounding board for the student. This team will only ask questions to guide the selection and justification of the solution.

Step Six: The student will write out his or her solution and present it to the class.

also helped to transfer newly discovered information into different situations and across the curriculum. Through inquiry, learning becomes engaging, interesting and practical.

Although inquiry is a process, process and content cannot be separated. Students are required to inquire into something. Inquiry is a sifting process whereby students look at information and evidence relevant to a problem solution and begin to evaluate and rank those alternatives which better satisfy bringing the problem to resolution (Frankel 1973). Given the opportunity to inquire, students will be able to read, study, analyze and synthesize information from a variety of sources. As this information is internalized, appropriate facts, concepts and solution alternatives will be recalled to support the conclusions that the student formulates.

As inquiry investigations proceed, students will sense the need for more information or evidence to support their ideas and beliefs (hypotheses). Large problems will generate subproblems which, in due course, will require investigation. As students move deeper into their investigations, the critical thinking skills characteristic of the inquiry method will be refined and utilized. Students will become more analytical and value-judging as they proceed. In the final steps of bringing the problem to resolution, evaluation, separating relevant from irrelevant data, checking the reliability of sources, and comparing and contrasting alternative solutions will play an important role. Students will also sense the need to narrow their investigations. Information will become more selective and point to the solutions which require support.

The teaching/learning signals in the inquiry classroom will not come from the teacher in a continuous onstage model as a presenter of information. Students will have the responsibility of generating problems and explaining information and solution alternatives. The teacher skills will move to facilitating and skill coaching, motivating and inspiring students to become involved in their own educational development and learning. Teachers will encourage cooperative learning and maintain the momentum and rhythm of inquiry within the classroom.

Because inquiry is a process involving a combination of skills (processes) that are designed to confront a problem, define it, separate relevant from irrelevant information related to the problem, explore competing alternatives, and choose a solution that best resolves the prob-

Figure 5.7: Infusing Critical Thinking Skills
Into the Inquiry Process

The student is confronted with a problem. The student then:

STEP ONE:

states the problem clearly, accurately, and in a simple way.

Skill Clusters:

Attributing: describing the characteristics of people, places, things, events, ideas, etc.

Major related skill: Comparing and Contrasting

STEP TWO:

reads background information relevant to the problem and is encouraged to construct a "tentative" answer to the problem (the word "hypothesis" or "proposition" may be used for "answer" but is not necessary).

Skill Clusters:

Attributing

Causal Explanation: Assessing how well new data fits what else we know.

Major related skill: Generalizing

STEP THREE:

investigates the problem and the tentative answer proposed. Alternative answers are discovered, explored, redefined and evaluated (tested).

Skill Clusters:

Attributing
Causal Explanation
Evaluating
Inferring: Making statements about the unknown on the basis on the known.

Major related skill: Analyzing

Figure 5.7 continued

STEP FOUR:

> *formulates* a final solution (conclusion) to the problem and states "why" (reasons) for this solution
>
> *Skill Clusters:*
> **Inferring**
> **Causal Explanation**
> *Major related skill:* Explaining
> **Evaluating**
> *Major related skill:* Making decisions, generalizing

STEP FIVE:

> *reviews* the entire process with a learning team who serve as a sounding board for the inquirer. This team will ask questions causing the inquirer to reassess h/her final solution.
>
> *Skill Clusters:*
> **Evaluating**
> **Causal Explanation**

STEP SIX:

> *writes* out his or her solution and presents it to the class.

---

lem, it is imperative that skills coaching become a major pedagogical focus. The critical thinking skills in this chapter (also refer to the *Effective Thinking Skills Model,* 4–6, page 25), when learned and practiced by students, will greatly facilitate the inquiry process.

In Figure 5.7, these skills are again summarized and interwoven with the steps of the inquiry model. This chart will serve as a quick reminder for the teacher of when and where certain basic thinking skills can be infused into the inquiry process. In this manual it is impossible to duplicate the variety of "teachable" moments related to elementary inquiry teaching. That being said, it will be through continual and consistent practice that teachers will improve the inquiry thinking capabilities of students.

EVALUATING INQUIRY

The evaluation of an inquiry lesson is always needed; yet, the classroom evaluation of problem solving and inquiry activities is often neglected. Here are some reasons for such neglect:

1. Inquiry lessons are process oriented and cannot be tested by a simple objective test.
2. Inquiry lessons involve human interactions that are more complex than separate bits of information. They do not lend themselves to the assessment of narrow, isolated skills.
3. Many times objective tests are extremely artificial and isolated, totally foreign to real-life investigations. These tests sometimes obscure the real purpose of inquiry and what the student actually has accomplished.
4. Inquiry lessons are open-ended and have flexible answers. It is more difficult to write tests for an inquiry lesson than for a lesson based on preconceived teacher expectations.

How then can teachers evaluate inquiry lessons with positive results? Here are four suggestions:

1. Sometimes we overlook the obvious. In the course of an investigation, students will draw pictures, maps, graphs, charts or diagrams, or create models and displays. Sometimes they are required to write letters, complete an interview, or make an oral presentation. When this work is collected, analyzed and displayed, it has the potential of making evaluation and diagnosis practical and meaningful.
2. Personal interviews with students, although time consuming, will also be useful especially for those whose reading or writing skills are limited. An interview provides the teacher with diagnostic information as well as summative information.
3. During an inquiry lesson, students will spend much time in group work and other non-paper and pencil activities. Direct teacher observation of pupil behaviors is a valuable method of determining to what extent students are using certain learning and human relation skills in their problem investigations.
4. Finally, it is sometimes beneficial to ask students what they

think they are learning. "I learn" statements can be revealing. Their strength is that they represent pupil-initiated responses and do not require the student to focus on a preconceived "right" answer (Armstrong 1977).

One method of assisting students evaluate what they have learned in an inquiry lesson is the **checklist**. Checklists will enable teachers to identify basic skills and the extent of their use by students. By keeping the checklist up to date during an inquiry unit of study, a teacher will be able to diagnose both individual and group progress in the use of fundamental inquiry and critical thinking skills. The checklist example below (Figure 5.8) will help you with your evaluations (Ellis et al. 1977).

Figure 5.8: Inquiry Skills Checklist

Student Name: ______________________

Student Behaviors	COMPLETED PROJECTS *P1*	*P2*	*P3*	*P4*	*P5*	*P6*	*P7*	*P8*	*P9*	*P10*
Specific Skills Checklist										
Asks Questions										
Draws maps										
Makes observations										
Makes graphs										
Draws sketches										
Makes measurements										
Records data										
Research Skills Checklist										
Locates sources of information										
Conducts interviews										
Uses library effectively										
Uses Index, Table of Contents										
Gathers data from charts, tables, graphs, & maps										
Takes notes effectively										
Organizes diverse information										
Arranges ideas in logical order										
Is aware of biases in information										

Figure 5.8 continued

Student Name: _____

Student Behaviors	P1	P2	P3	P4	P5	P6	P7	P8	P9	P10
Concern for Others										
Is sensitive to the needs of others										
Helps others meet their needs										
Willingly shares ideas										
Willingly shares materials										
Accepts suggestions and help										
Makes constructive suggestions										
Sticks to group decisions										
Works cooperatively with others										
Gives others encouragement										
Respects property of others										
Appears to like group work										
Thinking Skills										
Attributing Comparing and Contrasting										
Causal explanation Explaining										
Inferring Analyzing										
Evaluating Generalizing										

Directions:

Rate specific skills relevant to each project as either (E) excellent, (G) good, (F) fair, or (N) not observed.

The specific thinking skill mastered should be noted on the chart. Several major thinking skills have been listed.

CHAPTER SIX

Operational Skills (Grades 7–12)

ᗏ

THE MIDDLE SCHOOL: THINKING IN TRANSITION

Problem solving is process oriented. This process is learned by confronting events, defining problems, puzzling with them, experimenting, trying different and unusual solution alternatives, and searching for the most effective answers. Problem solving and inquiry demand the total use of one's cognitive powers and all the resources one can command to search for solutions. Also, problem solving is best learned when confronting real problems, not artificial ones. As the level of problem solving application becomes more complex, theoretical and abstract, problem solving must call upon those skills associated with formal thinking. Teaching-for-thinking will differ as the cognitive level matures and as students make the transition from concrete to formal operations.

Because the methods used to teach children are indeed important and require our evaluation, we should begin to focus on teaching-for-thinking, which can be viewed as both an *end* and a *means* in the storehouse of educational goals and strategies used in the public schools. More particularly, "thinking" and "teaching-for-thinking" are justifiable pursuits of middle grade education. We now know that thinking—critically and creatively—is an important feature of productive societies (Torrance 1990). Futurists predict that in the next century schools must become "thinking" schools in order to survive, because the quality of life and work (its changing nature and complexity) emerging before us demands individuals who are flexible, creative and critical thinkers, who can solve societal, environmental and economic problems, and who can increase the quality of life in a world of growing hostility, a world where environmental resources are quickly being depleted.

Of course, teaching-for-thinking commits us to respect the intelligence of teachers and students. This is a practical, perhaps moral, lesson and one that is difficult to learn. Instructional improvement with an emphasis on intellectual processes is and should continue to be teacher-dependent and student-focused. When teachers begin to develop their own thinking and problem solving skills, they will be more apt to try new ideas in the classroom. Also, when teachers are learning and are given the freedom to be innovative, the curriculum becomes teacher-proof and the rewards of teaching intrinsic. Teachers with a vision to share usually speak that vision and act on it to create "learningful" classrooms.

Thinking In Transition

Like learning, thinking is incremental and developmental. This conclusion—based on knowledge of how students learn (Inhelder and Piaget 1964)—implies that some intellectual processes are more basic than others and are required for mastering more complex mental operations. This is not to imply that students naturally exhibit growth in thinking due to passing through the various cognitive stages as defined by Piaget. Rather, it implies that "mentally" or "intellectually" the student is naturally ready to perform cognitive functions at these levels (given that the student has normal brain function). Patricia Arlin (1987) reminds us:

> The classroom is the ideal place to provide the experiences that students need to develop formal thinking skills and concepts. Without planned experiences and developmentally based instruction, students do not appear to develop formal reasoning on their own. This should not be surprising since Inhelder and Piaget seemed to imply this in their definition of the eight formal schemata as: "...concepts which the subject potentially can organize from the beginning of the formal level when faced with certain kinds of data, but which are not manifest outside these conditions."

To say this is to remind ourselves that thinking at each significant developmental stage will not occur unless students have many opportunities to develop the thinking skills appropriate for each period of growth.

Arlin continues: "They are the tasks, the problems and the opportunities which are provided in the classroom for the students to experience what these concepts look like when they are used." The work of Patricia Arlin in defining "thinking levels" is grounded in the research of Piaget who observed that teaching-for-thinking is teaching for understanding, and we teach for understanding by supplying the repertoire of experiences and actions a student requires if s/he is to have the data to reflect upon and the data from which s/he will construct formal reasoning concepts.

The middle school educator, in order to teach-for-thinking, is therefore required to define the cognitive level(s) of middle grade youngsters (thinking in transition) and identify those appropriate methods and strategies that provide opportunities for cognitive growth. From this research, the assumption is made that middle school students are able to make some cognitive progress, especially if we are able to identify their transitional positions and the means by which to move them forward intellectually. Arlin (1987) states the following:

> If throughout our educational experience our concepts undergo these many different constructions depending on our stage and level of thinking, then the words of Philip Cowan suggest a way to begin to think about teaching for thinking and about a developmental curriculum, for, he says, "like the child the curriculum should follow a special course returning every few years to similar problem areas but each time requiring different structural levels of thought and action" (Cowan 1978, p 204).

According to Arlin, transitional thinking falls between the high concrete and low formal levels. **High concrete** thinking exhibits some evidence of a systematic approach to problems but gives no evidence of being able to form an abstraction from the problems. **Low Formal** thinking, on the other hand, gives clear evidence of some formal thinking (on the Arlin test, three to five of the eight formal concepts being present in their thinking). At the low formal level of cognitive ability, students are capable of abstraction and of making inferences but need to be provided opportunities to develop formal thinking operations.

Arlin's test results show that 60.25 percent of sixth through ninth graders are at the concrete level, 14.5 percent are in the transitional level, and 25.25 percent are at the level of formal reasoning. A closer examination shows that 47.5 percent are at the *high* concrete level and 21 percent are at the *low* formal level. The transitional level is described by Arlin as representing:

> ...performance on the formal tasks which is best described as providing evidence of a systematic approach to the problem and some use of abstraction and inferences but the performance is quite inconsistent. The subtest score patterns of students who receive transitional scores need to be analyzed individually to determine if the concrete or formal categories are best applied to their performance. If there is evidence of two or three of the formal concepts being present then the subject is showing some evidence of formal reasoning.

Utilizing Arlin's research and definition of "transitional thinking," we should be able to provide a solid base for constructing the cognitive (intellectual) parameters of a middle grades curriculum Recently, James A. Beane (1990) analyzed current efforts at defining "a middle school curriculum." To share with you Beane's conclusions is to point out the muddled curricular efforts aimed at defining what should and should not be taught in the middle level of school. Beane remarks: "Largely obscured in this search for improved middle level education has been what is probably the most critical question in this or any other kind of authentic school reform: What should be the curriculum of the middle school?"

After a cursory survey of middle level curricular proposals, Beane dismisses them in favor of a two-pronged approach to curricular reform—the intersection of personal concerns and social issues. He comments:

> In the intersections between these two categories, then, we may discover a promising way of conceptualizing a general education that serves the dual purpose of addressing the personal issues, needs, and problems of early adolescents and the concerns of the larger world, including the particular society in which they live. It is here that we may find themes that ought to drive the curriculum of the middle school as a general education program. And it is here that we may finally find a way of positioning subject matter so that it presents a justifiable and

compelling source of study for early adolescents and the adults who work with them.

Beane tells us that middle school curricular reform should include structural changes and a coherent/unifying curriculum. This last concept is defined by Beane as based upon (1) the interests of early adolescents"; (2) the "characteristics" of early adolescents; (3) the "needs" of early adolescents; and (4) as "general education" which is a combination of the personal and social concerns of the middle level student.

Beane outlines the general educational themes that *ought* to drive the curriculum. These themes include transitions, identities, interdependence, wellness, social structures, independence, conflict resolution, commercialism, justice, caring, and institutions. Thematic they are, but they read more like the contents of a social psychology text than the stuff from which an academic curriculum is built. Beane does include "skills" in his reform curriculum: reflective thinking, critical ethics, valuing, self-concepting, social action, and the skill of searching for completeness and meaning. These are needed, he remarks, for exploring the aforementioned themes.

While seeking in my own work (*Philosophy for Young Thinkers* 1987) to build a concept-and value-based curriculum for middle level thinkers, I too used many of these same themes. But this curriculum sought a firmer foundation than just the affective needs, characteristics and interests of youngsters. I too felt the pull of society to develop a rigorous academic curriculum, but did not feel compelled to throw out traditional subject matter just because it was traditional. While Beane seeks a broad conceptual base for the middle school curriculum and is highly critical of what he labels the "narrow focus on fragmented subjects," he fails to understand that "subjects" are broad curriculum concepts, handed down through time and valued by society. In fact, his concern with current information about adolescent behavior has become the foundation for promoting a thematic and content thin middle level curriculum. I am not so sure that the society with which he wishes to intersect would agree that so-called traditional subject matter—language arts, social studies, science, and mathematics—should be squeezed into effectively controlled thematic units.

Of course, there is a reason for this weak curriculum emphasis in the middle school—the lack of a "research-based conceptualization and the benefits of a tough-minded theory" definitive of the so-called "middle school concept" (Paul George 1988). George, in recanting the history of the middle school movement, makes several interesting observations:

1. that from 1900–1960, the idea of the middle school emerged as a response to the needs of adolescents;
2. that from 1960-1980 middle school educators began to develop notions about appropriate school experiences for this age group;
3. that this last phase is genuinely insecure because it has not been tested and validated. This, says George, should be completed between 1980 and the year 2000. This will continue into the next century and George predicts: "Research in the area of human growth and development will have established the crucial nature of early adolescence in our culture, and affirmed the importance and effectiveness of fully functioning middle schools in assisting the passage from childhood to adolescence or young adulthood."

The lack of a firm research base for the building of a middle level curriculum has been a definite problem for middle school curricula builders. This has led to a strong emphasis being placed on "self-esteem" by middle level educators. This emphasis has in fact been the driving force behind the middle school movement. George reflects that the middle school movement is "one of the few humanistic innovations brought on the scene since the Progressive Education movement that is still thriving and growing." In a survey of middle schools, Joyce L. Epstein (1990) found that "those schools dedicated exclusively to the middle grades…assigned high priority to the goal of personal growth and the development of self-esteem."

Although there is nothing a priorily wrong with emphasizing the affective needs of the learner at any level of schooling, these needs are incapable of driving a content-based curriculum that prepares youth for a world of competition and complexity.

Hershel Thornburg (1988) provides some clues for building and maintaining an effective middle level curriculum. He actually offers a definition of "transitional" as applied to the middle school student. Thornburg's description embodies three theoretical concepts: physical development, cognitive development and social development. Two insights characterize Thornburg's research that are important to developing a middle level curriculum: (1) he maintains that "changes in the social environment or social interactions do not necessarily imply that the capacity of the individual has changed," and (2) he says that "once logic and reasoning are complete, one's mental skills might branch out depending on schooling, experiences, interests, motivations, and consistent exposure to ideas, objects or, as in school, subject matter."

The point is quite clear—the learner must gradually acquire a working vocabulary of abstract terms and relinquish h/her dependency on concrete-empirical props (Ausubel and Ausubel 1966). This occurs as the learner becomes familiar with school content (Mishra 1975) or subject matter (Bruner 1966). Thronburg says that "...all these processes should begin to occur between 11–13 years of age, the range Inhelder and Piaget (1958) called transitional thought."

Conrad Toepfer (1989) agrees that "we should provide learning opportunities that appropriatey challenge early adolescents." He further comments:

> Middle level G/T programs can make good use of the Arlin Test. It can identify whether a youngster is a low concrete, high concrete, low formal, or high formal level thinker. It is helpful for identifying the readiness of youngsters to perform the particular thinking levels required to understand and process the cognitive level demands of specific subjects.

Although these comments were meant to address academically gifted programs at the middle level of schooling, they certainly cannot be limited to students of high I.Q. Toepher adds: "In itself, I.Q. does not specify the learner's cognitive levels and thinking abilities. However, we often falsely assume that all high I.Q. students have achieved advanced cognitive thinking levels."

The need to identify "transitional" thinking is apparent. I believe that Arlin has provided a research base to begin this process. This base has the inherent possibility of becoming the foundation for building a middle level academic curriculum. Will this curriculum be content-oriented, based solely on the affective needs of youngsters, or a combination of both? Answers to this question do not lie in cognitive research. Rather, this question—which lies at the heart of the middle school movement—will be based on reason as it impacts on tradition, cultural constraints, future needs, and the psycho-social characteristics of middle level youngsters.

Thinking as Problem Solving

An instructional bridge must be built that will help students in the middle make the transition from concrete to the early formal level of thinking. The characteristics of this bridge must reveal an openness to both concrete and formal thinking; that is, it must allow students to venture back and forth from the concrete to the formal and from the formal to the concrete as their thinking continues to mature. By allowing early formal thinking, this bridge will tend to pull students forward. By making provisions for both concrete and early formal thinking, it will allow the student to set his or her own individual pace and pattern of growth.

The transitional bridge we are searching for is found within the nature of thinking itself—thinking as "problem solving." Cognitive scientists (Hunt 1982; Newell and Simon 1972; Johnson-Laird 1983) define *thinking* as a problem solving process. We too have learned that a person is confronted with a problem when s/he wants to make sense out of some experience, or a bit of new information, or when s/he wants something and does not know immediately how to get it. Thinking is an effort to arrive at some desired goal; hence, thinking is problem solving. Johnson-Laird observes: "...thinking is not a thing, but a process...a continual movement back and forth from thought to word and from word to thought. Every thought tends to connect something with something else, to establish a relationship between things. Every thought moves, grows, and develops, fulfills a function, solves a problem."

When humans (students) are thought of as problem solvers, we are able to examine the steps leading to problem resolution and discover clues about the nature of human thinking, thinking skills and reasoning processes. This examination will guide our efforts in providing a transitional bridge for the teaching-for-thinking classroom.

When **thinking** is thought of as problem solving, we are able to isolate four fundamental cognitive operations characteristic of all learning operations. These operations were explicated in chapter one of this manual but are repeated here in the context of outlining the basic steps of problem solving as a learning tool for operating in one's environment.

1. **Perception and recognition.** A person perceives the raw data of experience and processes these perceptions, recognizing the patterns generated by memory, which allow the components of the problem to emerge. This knowledge forms the conceptual base for meaning and understanding.

2. **Organization.** In Johnson-Laird's view, "...every thought tends to connect something with something else, to establish a relationship between things." Organizational thinking is necessary for problem solving and will involve the skills of classification, seriation and sequencing. To be able to organize one's experiences is the ability to transform incoming information into one's problem space and identify gaps in data. It is also the ability to determine where one is in relationship to solving the problem or resolving the issue and what kinds of actions are required, to bring the problem situation to a close.

3. **Storage, retrieval and transformation of data.** The total set of mental operations—whether concrete, high concrete, transitional, low formal or high formal—is one's mental (intellectual) productive system. These are revealed in our approach to critical thinking: either data-driven or goal-driven. Data-driven cognitive processing is relatively automatic, less capacity-limited, and more open to a variety of inputs and processes. It is learned early in life and is therefore more primitive, yet more flexible, than goal-driven thinking. The nature of inquiry requires one to listen, perceive, and adjust one's thinking to the data offered by experience.

   Goal-driven cognitive processing requires conscious control, sets rules, and is more of the nature of formal thinking. Goal-driven thinking has severe capacity limitations, works in a serial capacity, and is usually begun as a response to internal signals. It is a goal-oriented, consciously learned behavior. Goal-driven thinking is found in such approaches as the scientific method, creative problem solving, research papers, and other process skills that require some formal reasoning.

4. **Reasoning.** In the course of carrying out a problem solving activity, the student will discover whether any steps or series of steps decreases the distance to the goal of problem resolution. If this occurs, the student will continue with it, but if not, the student will move on to other steps. If the entire program fails to carry one to the desired goal, the student can either quit, modify the process or change the problem itself. This requires a high level of reasoning ability and some that fall in the formal range—inductive and deductive inference, quantitative and qualitative analysis, and the ability to work in problem solving teams.

The above research data on "thinking-as-problem-solving" can be organized for instructional purposes in the following way:

1. Facilitating Skills, Grades K–3. These are the micro-thinking skills necessary for performing all other thinking operations. They are requisite for mastering basic subject-related skills (number operations, reading, writing, and research/comprehension skills). This stage is characterized by perception and organization abilities—skills that are necessary for inferential thinking, predicting, and problem solving. Because younger children are primarily sensory-oriented, learning should include as many hands-on activities as possible and be discovery-based. The basic organizational functions of this stage are classification, seriation and sequencing (Piaget 1926; Piaget and Inhelder 1969; Lowery 1989; Sternberg 1979; Inhelder and Piaget 1964; Langford 1989; Whiteley 1985).

2. Processing Skills, Grades 4-6. At this stage students are able to process ideas simultaneously and group them according to multiple attributes (subordinate/superordinate relationships). They now are able to conserve quantity, length and number while grouping and can process multiple properties and concepts at the same time (a movement into high concrete thinking). Now they able to develop the skill of reversibility—undo operations mentally—permitting the thoughtful exploration of various procedures with the ability to return to the beginning wherever and whenever necessary. They now can use words and symbols to stand for concrete objects, lifting them from the strict limitations of early concrete thinking and setting the stage for the transition to formal operations.

Processing skills, when placed in the curriculum, support and extend the skill combinations required for inquiry thinking, leading to more formal reasoning and problem solving. It is now that the curriculum should become more conceptually and process-based with factual content called upon to explain and extend the understanding of concepts. Inquiry includes explaining, using multiple descriptors and cause/effect relationships, forming hypotheses, interpreting and drawing conclusions, evaluating and classifying relationships, utilizing analogy and metaphor, and creating two-and three-dimensional models.

Although inquiry processes at this level resemble problem solving and include many similar procedures, there is a fundamental difference—problem solving requires the ability to reason abstractly, utilize propositional thinking, and make logical deductions. Inquiry, on the other hand, is tied to concrete thinking, factual information and discovery (inductive) learning. Inquiry is less formal, less structured, and utilizes sensory inputs and experiential learning. At this point, fully developed formal reason is not required. Inquiry also includes concept analysis (tied to concrete examples and situations), simple inferences, evaluation using multiple descriptors, and the ability to understand simple analogies and metaphors.

3. Operational Skills, Transitional to Formal, Grades 7–12. Operational skills are characterized by abstract and propositional thinking. At the high end, this includes the ability to utilize formal reasoning and formal problem solving procedures. At the low end, this includes the beginning of the problem solving, inferential process. Students are now learning to use thoughts, ideas and concepts and are pulling away from relying on their concrete (limited) referents. Thought is now being brought to bear on multiple possibilities in order to explore the many alternative hypotheses that lie before them.

A characteristic of this stage is combinatorial reasoning. Students will begin to organize, reorganize and apply purpose to process and product. Thinking will become more goal-oriented as learning is focused on goals and objectives. As they move from high concrete to early formal reasoning, students should be encouraged to become more flexible in their judgments and tolerant of ambiguities, keeping in mind that solutions, facts, values and methods of knowing change from time to time and, perhaps, from culture to culture.

As solution-alternatives present themselves, students will begin evaluating alternatives using traditionally established criteria. As formal reasoning occurs, they will create their own criteria for making judgments. Although students are in transition from concrete to formal thinking, abstract and propositional skills will not occur naturally. These skills must be taught, practiced, refined and reinforced (Piaget 1978) if they are to become a part of the student's repertoire of thinking skills. We should remember the caution of Patricia Arlin: "Without planned experiences and developmentally based instruction, students do not appear to develop formal reasoning on their own."

The data base now available through cognitive scientists and developmental psychologists, as well as those who have done extensive research on middle level students, provides a conceptual base for organizing or reorganizing middle school teaching and learning. The middle school student represents a mixed lot, perhaps more interested in social and personal growth than in cognitive/academic areas. This should not deter us from developing rigorous academic curricula, but it should sensitize us to the reality of the middle school child. For the teacher this means that classrooms will be characterized by a wide range of interests and intellectual abilities. It also implies that no single teaching method will always "work" for the improvement of learning at this age. The teachers in the middle must be aware of teaching and learning styles, of creative and innovative methods, and not be afraid to explore new ways to approach middle school teaching. Above all, teachers should understand middle level student needs, be prepared to individualize instruction, and become sensitive to emerging (transitional) intellectual needs. This procedure will help attend to the self esteem of the middle school child as much as cooperative learning, peer tutoring, teaming, and flexible grouping patterns. Experience tells us that one way of attending to self esteem is to allow learning to occur. This will happen when we do not "undershoot" or "overshoot" the transitional range of the middle schoolers' intellectual functioning.

Experience has taught us that middle level students are capable of learning at much higher levels than was previously thought. What we must do, if we are to reach every student we teach, is to incorporate into every lesson, every day, those skills, concepts, facts and values which interest and motivate, as well as those which challenge the student intellectually. Teaching-for-thinking can be accomplished in the middle school if we identify those skills and skill combinations which are able to bridge the gap between the concrete and formal levels of thought. We want middle level students to have confidence in their emerging abilities. We can accomplish this goal by identifying their general cognitive readiness levels to which we match our instruction. Toepfer (1989) comments: "Herman Epstein (1981) observed that cognitive levels matching can identify and diagnose student cognitive levels, and organize learning activities matched with student readiness to learn facts and information. Such appropriate challenges can help students consolidate their manifested skills while initiating new ones as their readiness allows. Matching the level of learning challenge with demonstrated student cognitive level readiness can minimize inappropriate learning challenges."

THE METHOD OF PROBLEM SOLVING

Background

Problem solving, when performed in a systematic and consistent fashion, creates a special and consequential interaction between the student and his or her environment. Problem solving is an activity when engages and stimulates the learner in the movement toward problem and/or conflict resolution. It requires mental alertness and an uncommon interest in the world in all of its varied and interesting manifestations. Problem solving requires a sense of timing and an intuitive relationship with the task-environment. While engaged in problem solving, nothing is able to replace an interest in one's task, a desire to resolve complicated and perplexing issues, and a broad base of knowledge and interest.

Problem solving requires an interaction of the learner with sometimes raw, uninterpreted information and the ability to recognize the different components of the problem as they appear out of context and in different ways. Problem solving is based on the ability to adapt ourselves, consciously and deliberately, to situations we have not found before and for which we have no ready-made response.

Problem solving will involve all of the critical thinking skills and subskills that we have studied so far. As the subject of problem solving grows more technical and the students become more mentally mature, they will be required to solve problems formally and abstractly through the use of formal operational skills, mathematics and logic. The purpose of teaching for discovery, inquiry and problem solving is to allow students to mature—developmentally—from the preoperational stage through the concrete and formal operational stages of thinking.

We should never forget that effective problem solving requires the learning of not only critical thinking skills, but also the skills, concepts and facts associated with a wide variety of subjects as well. This will involve the skills of concept analysis and hypothesis testing, and the discipline of research and logical consistency in finding new solutions to contemporary problems.

> It was through critical judgment that humans arose from savagery to civilization and this is also the means by which civilizations improve.

Knowledge is a living organism. It is not a static inventory that can be divided into facts, values, departments or courses of study. These areas represent the application of tradition and order to that which defies definition. Such an interpretation reflects our biases—those associated with Western Civilization—and tends to harden our own mental encapsulation, preventing us from "seeing" the world through the eyes and understanding of others. This living organism of knowledge is forever changing and growing. Within the presence of constant change, critical judgment is necessary. It is not a luxury.

What happens when we are confronted with a problem that blocks customary patterns of thinking and believing? Mental flexibility is required in the application of critical thinking to new situations as we try to "flesh" out competing and alternating solutions to problems. As we organize these puzzles into hypothoses, propositions and possible solutions, the challenge is to assist our students in arriving at more and better answers and not to stifle their mental creativity with our own professional narrowness and traditions.

When problem solving and critical thinking are working best, they are creative processes. We can teach students the method: how to recognize problems, how to state problems in a useful manner, how to write hypotheses, how to test them, how to sift through alternative solutions, how to arrive at conclusions, and how to write these conclusions plainly and present them to others. These steps by themselves will not produce effective problem solvers. Behind most creative leaps of the imagination is some ineffable process resulting from a person's particular knowledge base (his or her cognitive and religious beliefs, morals, and social and family traditions). Important is the way in which a person mentally organizes his or her problem within that knowledge base and the freedom s/he feels to arrange and rearrange problems, interpret goals, "see" new relationships, comprehend the behaviors needed to get to a solution, and make the cognitive leaps that characterize creative discovery and invention. Teacher modeling is essential as these processes begin to occur.

Creativity, meaning and understanding enhance problem solving. They account for the power of analogical reasoning, the use of the familiar to understand the unfamiliar, and to compare and contrast at a metaphorical level. It is through metaphor that we are able to connect disparate clusters of information to form new and illuminating concepts and meanings. Analogy and metaphor are creative processes which deepen our understanding, analytical abilities, and the skill of "seeing" new patterns and relationships among the new, as well as the old, knowledges. We cannot overestimate the power of analogy and metaphor in finding new solutions to old problems, opening new avenues of thought that enable us to pursue likenesses and differences, organizing our understandings into broad conceptual patterns, and discovering new meanings and understandings.

Becoming Better Problem Solvers

1. Students need to create a knowledge base through reading and studying a wide variety of subjects and books. Knowledge provides the basis for recognizing the components of a problem, seeing relationships and making comparisons. Without a knowledge base, no solution alternatives can be generated.

2. Creative problem solving often flourishes in isolation. Aloneness sometimes helps a person listen to the inner self. Creative ideas are likely to emerge from incubation during a period of inactivity when the barriers to unconscious processing are down.

3. Middle and high school students will usually tackle a problem at a high level of abstraction. This will avoid getting mentally locked into one point of view or stream of thought. Abstractness increases objectivity by enabling the student to pull back from the many subproblems generated by emotion and enabling the student to reconsider remote and unlikely points of view.

4. Problem solving will be enhanced when students are encouraged to think in terms of broad categories (basic attributes), causal explanations, consistent and inconsistent solution implications, and the value of certain solution alternatives for problem resolution. Concept exploration is essential and should occur daily. When teaching the process of problem solving, overuse the action verbs definitive of the problem solving process. These verbs stress functions, and are more fluid and flexible than nouns. Thinking only in nouns reinforces rigid thinking and classifications.

Method

The method of problem solving is similar to that of inquiry. The differences stressed in this manual are primarily developmental. That is, at the elementary level, the inquiry method will be locked into concrete operations, especially for grades 2–6. As students move into the higher stages of concrete thinking, they will begin using abstract reasoning, though inconsistently. During the middle school years we discover that some students are concrete thinkers and that some are in the early stages of formal thinking. Also, there is another group that is neither concrete nor abstract. They are in transition and will demonstrate an inconsistent use of formal skills. For some, the stage of transition will last into adulthood; some will never rise to the level of formal operations. We should not accept this conclusion as final for, if instructed properly, students will be able to move fluidly from the stage of concrete to that of formal operations.

We can help improve thinking for this age group through problem solving. All of us think. This is a foregone fact. The problem is that most of our thoughts are rambling and undirected. Problem solving, when consistently used by teachers, will help improve the thinking of our students; it will especially assist those students whose thinking is in transition from concrete to formal operations.

The *Effective Thinking Skills Model, 7–12* (Figure 1.5) points out that the two organizing principles of problem solving are (1) abstract reasoning, the ability to use thoughts and ideas that have no immediate concrete referent, and (2) propositional thinking, bringing judgment–evaluation–logic to bear on statements embodied in propositions that claim factual status. These two principles are included in the problem solving process. But we should not expect middle school students, or even high school students, to use abstract and propositional reasoning consistently. The use of the problem solving method, with a gradual infusion of abstract and propositional thinking into the critical thinking skills definitive of the concrete level, will assist students with their cognitive transition.

It will be necessary for the teacher to judge when a student is *ready* to move from concrete to formal thinking. Today, the middle and high school teacher can use the Arlin Test (1987) to assist with this judgment. This test is developmental and is based on eight formal thinking operations. When a student lacks the ability to use formal operations consistently, the teacher can be sure that student is in transition from concrete to formal operations. The appropriate critical thinking skills should be applied to the level of the student with formal operations being introduced for instructional and cognitive growth purposes. The assessment of the student's cognitive level is a necessary step to instructional success. When accurate assessment is missing, we can never be sure if our instructional input is below or above the level of the student's cognitive reach. We should aim our instruction at the growing edge of student ability and be ready to remediate student deficiencies when and where they occur. Also, when skill mastery has occurred, we should provide ample enrichment opportunities which strengthen and fine tune the application of the skill in different contexts and with different content.

There are three fundamental steps in the problem solving process:

Step One: The Analysis of Problems

1. **Recognizing a problem exists**. Recognizing that a problem exists means breaking away from routine thinking and being willing to tackle the problems and issues that disturb normal thinking. As we are aware, most daily events are not earth-shaking and the routine adjustments we make to most situations are habitual. The problem is that too much routine blocks the recognition of problems when they occur. The willingness to recognize a problem is the beginning of critical thinking. Critical thinking will help clear away indecision and uncertainty by enacting changes in habitual thinking. Such a willingness will make a person more responsive to life's changing realities and provide more alternatives for behavior than were ever before imaginable. This is a first step—pre-step—to problem solving. Before problem solving can occur, a person must first acknowledge that s/he has a problem.

2. **Identifying a problem**. Once a student recognizes that a problem exists, the next step is to identify what kind of problem it is. A problem may fall into one of the following general groups:

a. **A problem of identification.** This problem arises when one needs to characterize a problem more explicitly, that is, when one needs to distinguish it from other ideas, concepts, situations, events, or things.

b. **A problem of causation.** This problem arises out of the need to discover a pattern in events so that we can trace backwards to a cause or forward to a conceived logical implication. One's ability to control h/her environment is dependent on h/her perception of such patterns and the ability to link a succession of events.

c. **A problem of means.** A problem of means concerns the wherewithal necessary to bring about a result conceived by the problem solver as a desirable state of affairs. The concern is how to get from where one is now to some preconceived point in the future.

d. **A problem of ends.** Sometimes one is uncertain of his or her goals. Alternatives are confusing and one feels that some things and not others are more worthy of pursuing. Uncertainty about ends may arise because some feel their experiences of attaining a goal were not what they expected them to be.

3. Stating a problem clearly. It is important for the problem solver to render a clearly conceived statement of the problem under investigation. A clearly stated problem will assist with communication during the problem solving process. Communication will be less confusing as ideas, methods, alternatives and solutions are presented, analyzed, utilized or discarded. A problem stated with clarity will enlist help from other individuals, help understand clues to action, and determine when the problem is solved.

4 Stating a problem usefully. In order to solve it, the problem must be formulated in accordance with one's abilities and resources for solving it. The problem-statement indicates the direction in which a solution might be found. A well-stated problem is a problem half-solved—that is, if there is a solution. One must remember that not every problem has a solution!

Step Two: The Formation of Hypotheses

The formation of hypotheses, as well as the other steps in critical thinking, must not be assumed to be distinct from the analysis of problems, either chronologically or logically. Although we are obliged to treat problem solving systematically, critical thinking does not necessarily follow an irreversible step-by-step process. We must understand the organic nature of critical thought, the impact of creative thinking, the involvement of experience and its extension through intuition, and the ability of students to range back and forth through each problem solving step.

The following processes are involving in producing hypotheses:

1. Collecting information. Collecting information begins with the identification of relevant material. More information will be read, summarized and categorized than will ever be needed or utilized. The student needs to understand that s/he can be more insightful and inventive when building on a foundation set by others. Research is necessary for effective problem solving to occur. Choosing information from one's collection will require reason and careful attention to the nuances of the problem to be solved.

2. Making information manageable. The second task is making the relevant information which the student has discovered manageable. Problems are not solved by merely collecting information and requiring students to use a set number of resources with note cards in hand. Too many students have been taught the art of copying from books and periodicals. Being able to quote facts and supposed authorities does not make one a critical thinker. It may make one a "critical memorizer" but holding thought in memory is not the same as applying critical judgment to it. The information upon which one bases solutions must be related to the problem under consideration either logically, causally or categorically. The ability to make connections in information is essential to adequate hypothesis production.

3. Writing the hypothesis. Hypotheses are only "possible answers" to a problem. The word "hypothesis" comes from two Greek words meaning "to place under." *When placed under the ordered and relevant information, the hypothesis gives a rational explanation for a state of affairs.* Many students are asked to formulate a hypothesis to which their research is to be addressed. This is called a **proto-hypothesis**. Proto-hypotheses help us collect and organize information. Whereas the proto-hypothesis is assumed, the actual hypothesis is consciously and deliberately formulated and based on the factual information (and its implications) developed by relevant research. The hypothesis actually functions as a proto-conclusion. That is, it is a possible conclusion which, if it survives examination and testing, becomes the conclusion to the problem. As Isaac Newton reflected, all scientific research must be restricted to the world of experience, tested and shared.

Hypotheses have the following characteristics:

a. Hypotheses appear only in the context of a problem.
b. Hypotheses do not appear in the absence of information and are not, therefore, based on an educated guess.
c. Hypotheses are found at the end of study and not at the inception of study.

Step Three: Examining and Testing Hypotheses

Critical thinking does not move neatly through clearly defined and separate steps. We have provided steps which will lead the student to state problems clearly and usefully, collect and organize information, and formulate hypotheses. But the critical thinker will seldom move smoothly through these steps and be ready, at this point, to examine and test his or her hypotheses. Rather, the problem solver will move forward and backward through the various problem solving steps. At any time, new information may be added, new hypotheses may be formed, and the problem may be redefined based on newly acquired evidence.

Without committing ourselves to a rigorous chronological ordering of the steps of the problem solving process, we can proceed to the five areas we have labeled "examining and testing hypotheses."

1. Recognizing assumptions. One looks backwards to locate assumptions. The assumptions are the intellectual background of a line of thought. They are foundational, yet they may not be stated, only assumed. Clarity demands that we identify hidden assumptions. These may be the **causal explanations** for certain events or ideas and beliefs. The relation of assumptions to argument is analogous to the relation of prejudice to human relations; they may be especially vicious when they play their roles without being noticed, but when brought into the open, they can be controlled.

2. Developing implications. A hypothesis should be plausible; it should not be a conjectural explanation of the phenomenon in question. Other requirements for hypotheses are that they must be capable of proof or disproof, adequate, involve no contradiction, and should be as simple as possible. Deduction is a human alternative to animal trial and error. Man elaborates mentally the consequences of hypotheses. He does not have to act upon every idea in order to determine its implications. The logical implications of a hypothesis should be considered and reconsidered before the hypothesis is itself accepted as final.

3. Examining implications. The implications of a hypothesis must be examined deductively and inductively. That a certain line of reasoning leads to a logical conclusion, a conclusion that is unwanted, should tell us that we have developed a hypothesis that does not suit our purposes. There may be conceptual errors within the hypothesis itself, the hypothesis may need complete reformulation, or we may need to re-examine our desired outcomes.

4. Interpreting observations. Hypotheses can be tested by making observations and conducting experiments. As we make observations we must continually apply reason to what is "seen." There is no such item in our experience as a "pure observation." To observations we bring assumptions and apply critical thinking. All observations are interpreted by us and given meaning and understanding via our repertoire of past experiences and common sense beliefs. In research and problem solving, nothing can be taken for granted. Facts, assumptions, hypotheses, observations and interpretations must be checked and rechecked for accuracy and logical consistency.

5 Drawing conclusions. The conclusion of our research is the hypothesis that survives examination and testing. The hypothesis which is the result of our research will always remain hypothetical even though it is the conclusion. It is the best answer at the present time to the problem that generated the inquiry. This conclusion is not the final answer because new information will always appear, causing us to reconsider the results of our inquiry. A solution deals with the problem. The conclusion to the problem is any means by which a problem ceases to be a problem. Still, conclusions are seldom, if ever, absolutely final in that all factual information is contingent and open to further investigation.

Strategy Focus

It is not enough that students are able to follow the problem solving process step-by-step. They must also know *when* to use each step and the **strategy focus** at each stage of development. Teachers will improve student performance in problem solving by teaching students how to recognize problems that require particular strategies. Because problem solving is a process or combination of critical thinking skills organized to solve a problem or reach a conclusion, there are certain critical thinking strategies through which we are able to approach problems to maximize our problem solving efforts. Teaching these will help students focus their efforts and use certain basic thinking skills in coping with everyday events and situations.

1. Analysis. If our purpose is analysis, then problem solving will be applied to ideas, relationships and concepts. Analysis seeks to clarify relationships, the meaning of words, and the implications of concept-applications. In analysis, the student should give careful attention to language habits and belief-assumptions. The student must be sensitive to the implications of tradition and search for coherence and consistency in all statements of belief and fact.

2. The comparative approach. The comparative approach brings into focus both the problem and its variety of proposed solutions. The comparative approach will help students sort and sift significant information when taking into account the analytic, descriptive, causal-explanatory and evaluative decisions made during the process. This method will assist students in reformulating questions and subproblems in order to arrive at more coherent and workable alternative solutions. This approach does not merely compare differences and similarities, consistencies and inconsistencies, but also focuses attention on *significant* differences, similarities, consistencies and inconsistencies within a problem set.

3. The descriptive method. Descriptions may either refer to knowing what is going on, what is the case, or what is true in a given instance. It also lifts **interpretations** to factual status rather than as ancillary to it. Interpretive elements (considered as "factual") used in descriptive contexts are such theoretical concepts as "cause and effect," "relationship," "thinking," "thought," "values," and "preferences." These ideas are non-factual and remain—in Kant's words—the contribution of the mind to the world of sensory experience. Through interpretation new experiences are related, organized and given meaning in the context of what we already know. They help us "verify" the statements made from our observations and experiences as "true or false," "valid or invalid."

4. The causal-explanatory method. Causality is usually associated with scientific judgment and experimentations. We should not confuse causality with meaning or the judgment of truth or worth. On the other hand, a **causal explanation** does assist the understanding of certain events and things, but one cannot substitute "what causes a behavior" with its "truth or worth." Explanation involves students in the search for clarity and the support of certain hypotheses and statements. We use the phrase "causal explanation" to refer to those ideas, facts, events, beliefs, behaviors, etc. that support or justify our conclusions or the effects that we perceive as events in the world.

5. The Evaluative Standpoint. Evaluation applies standards to the assessment of our propositions and solution alternatives. Evaluation will involve students in the process of setting criteria or standards in order to judge the results of problem solving, conclusions and recommendations. Because evaluation is selective, weighing, judgmental and appraising, it will be implicit in almost every step of the problem solving process. The criteria for evaluating the results of problem solving will result in a fusion of fundamental needs, values and aspirations with other truth seeking methods to reach a workable conclusion to our problem. Evaluation is a common sense guide to objectivity in that it forces us to *reconsider* all evidence presented when selecting a final solution to our problem.

FORMAL OPERATIONAL SKILLS

Patricia Arlin identifies eight concepts (skills) that developmentally define the stage of formal operations. These skills are tested by the *Arlin Test of Formal Reasoning* and demonstrate that when a student is unable to use these skills consistently, s/he is identified as either a concrete, high concrete or transitory thinker. The philosophy supportive of Arlin's research is that when students receive instruction in critical and formal thinking, they should demonstrate cognitive growth which is defined as being able to use these formal skills. Figure 6.1 identifies the formal skill-concepts used by Arlin.

The importance of these eight concept-skills cannot be overstressed. They represent a new level of abstraction, of thinking about the possible as well as the actual, of making predictions, forming hypotheses and thinking scientifically, which sets the adolescent apart from the child with h/her dependence on purely concrete objects and referents for thinking. We must emphasize that before these skills can successfully be learned and utilized by the middle or high school age student, the basic concrete operations must have been taught. Inhelder and Piaget stress that it is only *in the face of appropriate data and experience* and not outside these conditions that these concept-skills will develop. The logical place to provide these "data" and "experiences" is in the classroom.

To bring perspective to our teaching of critical thinking and formal operational skills, Arlin has defined the five cognitive levels supported by developmental research. The teacher who wishes to include thinking

Figure 6.1: Formal Skill Concepts

Multiplicative compensations (volume) is the concept which supports the understanding that when there are two or more dimensions to be considered in a problem, gains or losses in one dimension are made up for by gains or losses in the other dimensions. An example of this is the concept of conservation of volume. Since volume problems involve three dimensions (length, height, width), the correct solution to a conservation of volume problem requires compensation in terms of these three dimensions. The concept of multiplicative compensations is required to understand density problems in general science, to analyze closed systems in economics or social science, or life cycle problems in ecology. A common question which requires this kind of thinking for its answer is: "If I make this change, what effect does this have on ...?"

Correlations is a concept that implies the ability of a student to conclude that there is or is not a causal relationship, whether negative or positive, and to explain the minority cases by inference of chance variables. Correlational reasoning leads to the conclusion that two events, variables, etc. are or are not related and, in more sophisticated situations, determines the strength of that relationship. Correlation is used to determine the relationship of the amount of sunlight to plant growth, the relationship of the world market price of gold and international conflicts or inflation, or the relationship between working hard and getting good grades in school. Correlational reasoning provides answers to questions that begin: "What is the relationship between ...?"

Probability is a concept that supports the ability to develop a relationship between the confirming and the possible cases (especially when selecting between alternative solutions to a problem). Students use this concept whenever they figure the odds in games of chance, the likelihood that a particular political event will occur given several preconditions or scenarios, or the likelihood that the three remaining "Beatles" will ever make a new record together. Students are using this skill whenever they ask themselves the question: "What is the possibility that,...?" or "What is the likelihood that ...?"

Combinational reasoning involves the concept of generating all possible combinations of a given number of variables, choices, events, scenarios when a problem's solution requires that all possibilities be accounted for. Combinational thinking supports student reasoning about colors in art, problems in genetics, variations of ingredients in recipes and qualitative analysis problems in chemistry. Students use this concept when they ask the question: "What are all the possible combinations (arrangements, permutations) of ...?"

Figure 6.1 continued

Proportional reasoning is defined as a mathematical concept which involves the ability to discover the equality of two ratios which form a proportion. Map drawing skills, making drawings and models to scale presuppose proportional reasoning. This concept has implications for the arts and humanities as well. Aristotle defined an analogy as a statement where the second element is compared to the first as the fourth is to the third. Is this not a restatement of the definition of proportionality? Interpreting analogies and complex poetic examples requires multiple classifications and their coordination.

Forms of conservation beyond direct verification are more narrowly defined in terms of scientific concepts but they too have implications for other subjects in the curriculum. Forms of conservation beyond direct verification involve the ability to deduce and verify certain conservations by observing their effects and thus inferring their existence. No one has seen momentum; we only infer its existence from examples such as those observed on a pool table.

Mechanical equilibrium requires the ability to simultaneously make the distinction and the coordination of two complementary forms of reversibility—reciprocity and inversion. The idea of equilibrium suggests a system of trade-offs of multiple compensations. This concept represents the coordination of many different sets of compensations so that a balance or equilibrium is maintained. Hydraulics, pistons and similar types of problems in science require this type of thinking. Most economic theories require simultaneity and so do creating and interpreting formulas, writing novels, and the interpretation of complex plots.

The coordination of two or more systems or frames of reference is one of the most complex schemes, and yet its applications are wide-ranging. It may well be the scheme which acts as a bridging concept between formal and any type of post-formal thinking. This concept requires the ability to coordinate two systems, each involving a direct and an inverse operation, but with one of the systems in a relation of compensation or symmetry in terms of the other. It represents a type of relativity of thought. A common experience for persons flying in airplanes is to hear the pilot comment that their airspeed is 540 miles per hour but that their ground speed is 470 miles per hour. The two frames of reference for speed in this example are the work of the engine in the air and the progress that the plane is making relative to the ground being covered.

skill training in his or her classroom must be aware of these levels, discover where students are in their developmental growth, and teach appropriately. This will mean that teachers should offer instruction at their present level of thinking and, to provide growth in cognition, at the growing edge of their level in order to move them from concrete to formal thinking.

On the following pages is a summary of the steps of problem solving

Figure 6.2: Description of Arlin's Five Cognitive Levels

1. Concrete   This level represents performance by students on the formal tasks which is best described as providing no evidence of abstract reasoning and some difficulty with reasoning and skills that are problem specific.

2. High   This level represents performance on formal tasks which
   Concrete   is best described as providing some evidence of a systematic approach to problems but gives no evidence of being able to form a general rule or abstraction from the problems.

3. Transitional   This level represents performance on the formal tasks which is best described as providing evidence of a systematic approach to the problem and some use of abstractions and inferences but the performance is quite inconsistent. The subtest score patterns of students who receive transitional scores need to be analyzed individually to determine if the concrete or formal category is best applied to their performance. If there is evidence of two or three of the formal concepts being present, the subject is showing some evidence of formal reasoning.

4. Low Formal   This level represents performance on the formal tasks which gives evidence of three to five of the formal concepts being present in their thinking. They are capable of abstraction and making inferences but need to be provided with opportunities to develop thinking skills with respect to other formal concepts.

5. High Formal   This level represents performance on the formal tasks which gives clear evidence that most of the formal concepts are evident in their thinking. Reinforcement of these concepts is still appropriate.

with suggested points where critical thinking and formal operations might be used with students. (Figure 6.3) It goes without saying that teacher judgment is critical. Accurate judgment will depend both on knowledge of skills and knowledge of student ability. The following account is therefore merely a suggestion for **skill infusion**. Much depends on the level of students and the sensitivity of teachers. Through study, practice and diligence, teachers will be able to utilize critical and formal operations appropriately and in ways that maximize the learning of students.

If our goal is student growth in ability, then students will not be punished or "graded down" for trying new skills. One should not expect mastery at first attempt. Training in critical thinking skills and learning how to transfer these skills across the curriculum and in one's life and vocation takes years. We are only asking that teachers begin this process and that students be given the opportunity for growth and development.

Figure 6.3: Infusing Operational Skills into Problem Solving

Preparatory Steps to Skill Infusion

The teacher should

1. Make yearly plans for problem solving opportunities and skill infusion.
2. Identify subject-content area problems for possible investigation.
3. Identify the major concepts related to these problems for concept lessons.
4. Identify multi-subject areas or relationships where problems overlap or demonstrate cross curriculum contacts. At these critical points thinking skills can be infused to increase skill transference ability.
5. Identify problem solving strategies and the steps that are to be used for each problem. If students have not been previously instructed in the problem solving method, the teacher may wish to focus on one step at a time early on in the school year.
6. Decide which skills and reasoning processes are to be taught with each lesson. While planning, teachers will select skills related to (1) student ability, (2) a planned skill sequence, and (3) the goals of each lesson.

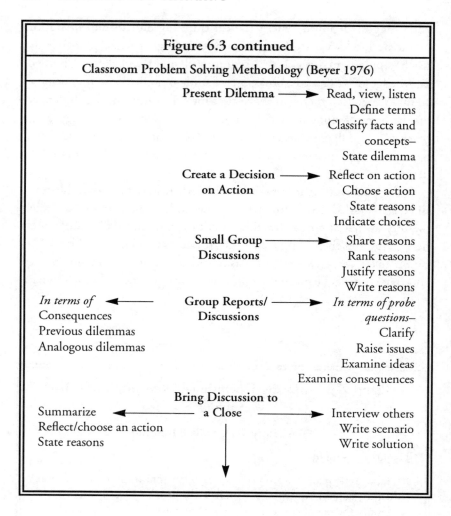

Figure 6.3 continued

Classroom Problem Solving Methodology (Beyer 1976)

Present Dilemma ——→ Read, view, listen
Define terms
Classify facts and
concepts–
State dilemma

Create a Decision ——→ Reflect on action
on Action Choose action
State reasons
Indicate choices

Small Group ——→ Share reasons
Discussions Rank reasons
Justify reasons
Write reasons

In terms of ←—— **Group Reports/** ——→ *In terms of probe*
Consequences **Discussions** *questions–*
Previous dilemmas Clarify
Analogous dilemmas Raise issues
Examine ideas
Examine consequences

Bring Discussion to
Summarize ←—— **a Close** ——→ Interview others
Reflect/choose an action Write scenario
State reasons Write solution

Figure 6.3 continued

Skill Infusion

STEP ONE: THE ANALYSIS OF PROBLEMS	STRATEGY FOCUS:

A. Recognizing a problem exists
 	
B. Identifying a problem
  •of identification
  •of causation
  •of means
  •of ends
 	
C. Stating the problem clearly
 	
D. Stating the problem usefully
	1. The **analysis** of the problem
	2. **Comparing** ideas and concepts
	3. **Describing** facts, events,
	   problems
	
	METHODOLOGY:
	  Present dilemma

Skill Infusion
Skill Cluster:

Attributing: describing the characteristics of people, places, things, events, ideas, problems, etc.

Related skills:

Comparing/contrasting
Classifying   Concrete to High
Sequencing   Concrete
Seriating

Major skill extension:

Comparing and Contrasting

Clarifying ideas
Finding significant similarities and differences
Finding significant patterns and concepts   Transitional
Interpreting significant similarities and differences

Formal Operational Skills

Multiplicative compensations
Correlations   Formal
Mechanical equilibrium
Coordination of frames of reference

Figure 6.3 continued

STEP TWO: THE FORMATION OF HYPOTHESES	STRATEGY FOCUS:

A. Collection information
 	
B. Making information manageable
 	
C. Writing the hypothesis
  •hypotheses appear in context
  •hypotheses appear with other information
  •hypotheses are rewritten at end of study
 	
D. Proto-hypotheses should be developed at the beginning of the investigation
	1. Comparing information
	2. Evaluating solution alternatives
	3. Explaining causal realtionships
	
	METHODOLOGY
	
	Create a decision on action
	
	Small group discussions

Skill Infusion

Skill Cluster:

Inferring: making statements about the unknown on the basis on the known.

Causal Explanation: assessing how well new data fits what else we know

Related skills:

Hypothesizing
Predicting
Generalizing
  (drawing a conclusion)
Analyzing relevant/irrelevant data
	Searching for causes
	Accounting for or against the
	  likelihood of a conclusion
	Assessing relevant evidence
	Explaining relationships

Major skill extension:

Analyzing	*Explaining*
Analyzing for bias Evaluating assumptions Checking for consistency Searching for causal relationships	Connecting pieces of evidence Gaining overall pictures Ranking rival conclusions Judging relevancy of information

Formal Operational Skills	Concrete to High Concrete
Probablility Combinational reasoning Forms of conservation beyond direct verification	Transitional Formal

Figure 6.3 continued	
STEP THREE: EXAMINING AND TESTING HYPOTHESES A. Recognizing assumptions B. Developing implications C. Examining implications D. Interpreting observations E. Drawing conclusions	STRATEGY FOCUS: 1. **Evaluating** solution alternatives 2. **Comparing** conclusions/answers 3. **Explaining** causal relationships METHODOLOGY 1. Group reports and decisions 2. Closure

Skill Infusion
Skill Clusters:

Evaluating: expressing approval or disapproval for alternative solutions.

Related skills:

Prioritizing
Assessing the relaibility of evidence   Concrete to
Establishing criteria of valuation   High
Generalizing   Concrete
Making decisions

Major skill extension:

Generalizing

Formulating hypotheses   Transitional
Stating obersevation reports
Testing observations for accuracy
Formulating generalization

Formal Operational Skills

Proportional reasoning (using metaphor and analogy)
Forms of conservation beyond direct verification
 (deduction and verification)   Formal
Coordination of two or more systems (frames or
 reference)
Coordination of frames of reference

PART THREE

Organizing School and Class for Teaching-For-Thinking

The application of thinking skills in the classroom requires training, patience and hard work on the part of the teacher. It goes without saying that theory without practice is of little value. Once we have mastered the skills of thinking for ourselves, the next task is that of organizing our schools and classrooms for thinking skills infusion. Richard Paul (1989) reminds us that a principal goal of critical thinking "is to help teachers learn how to teach it." His extensive research into teaching critical thinking helps teachers develop general strategies which can be used in the classroom setting and assists teachers in remodeling lessons for critical thinking skills infusion. He says the "...method of infusing instruction for critical thinking is the main concern..."of his work.

Knowing what one is doing is an essential element in being given credit or held responsible for one's actions. In order to help teachers get started with fostering the development of critical thinking and conceptual understanding in children, it may be necessary to turn to programs that have been written for these purposes. Learning from others may help us redevelop our own teaching and become more consistent in our teaching-for-thinking.

Chapter seven outlines several programs (or philosophies) that have been developed in recent years which enhance teaching for thinking. These include: *Philosophy For Young Thinkers, The Whole Language Movement, Future Problem Solving, The Scientific Method,* and *The Paideia Proposal.* If we can learn from these programs, then we too will be able to build a conceptual base of our own which emphasizes thinking skills, conceptual development and problem solving processes.

Chapter eight will help teachers and principals build a thinking skills program in their own schools. In this chapter is outlined the philosophy, goals and objectives of a sound thinking skills program. Ideas are given to help develop and evaluate a program of critical thinking. This chapter is presented in outline form and is intended to be used as a checklist of ideas and steps in organizing for thinking skills infusion.

Part three will include summaries of each thinking skill and thinking process used in this manual (graphically illustrated), and a glossary of key (technical) terms used in each chapter. These additions were suggested by teachers. They can be used for quick reference and for ideas for thinking skills infusion. The teachers who reviewed my original manuscript thought that these additions would make the book more usable for classroom planning and instruction.

CHAPTER SEVEN
Curricular Modifications

℘

PHILOSOPHY FOR YOUNG THINKERS

The *Philosophy For Young Thinkers* (1983) curriculum written by Joseph P. Hester and Philip F. Vincent, is an attempt to meet the requirements of the following educational demands:

1. In the future, only the process aspects of curriculum will meet the criteria essential to prepare youth for the world they will inherit.
2. The new goal for education should be the development of intelligent persons who will be able to solve the emerging problems of human social living.
3. Problem solving is best learned when confronting real problems, not artificial ones.
4. A future of choices requires persons who can solve problems and possess the positive human values that allow them to make intelligent evaluations and decisions.
5. Education for a future of change will always remain incomplete and open- ended. Thus, opportunities for learning must be available at any time in a student's life.

The first edition of *PYT* was published in 1983 as a guide for teachers wishing to restructure their teaching to include more in depth conceptual exercises and methods which require a high degree of critical analysis. In 1984, a companion volume, concentrating on problem solving and cooperative learning in the area of ethical values, was published entitled *Cartoons for Thinking*. Since 1984, *PYT* and *CFT* have been published in a revised second edition. Also, student workbooks beginning at the kindergarten level and ranging into the secondary level have been published. Teacher guides have also been published at the primary, elementary and middle school levels.

The *PYT* curriculum provides a systematically and developmentally sequenced program of concepts, skills and problem solving scenarios designed to engage students at appropriate levels of mental maturity and provides for them needed study at the higher levels of cognitive thinking. Using this curriculum on a regular basis, teachers will be able to encourage students to express their own philosophical ideas, images and feelings. Student thought processes will be challenged in inquiry and problem solving activities that take into account their cognitive development.

Utilizing a developmental approach to learning philosophical ideas and discussing philosophical problems, the *PYT* curriculum first identified the concepts and processes to be learned, and then organized these into a developmental sequence to provide for maximum learning, skill infusion and the creation of a skill-concept hierarchy.

Primary Level

Getting Acquainted with Philosophy is based on discovery learning which is concrete but thoughtful. The goals of this curriculum are the following:

1. To stimulate the young child's imagination, permitting h/her to think in words, pictures, and through music, dance, and drama.
2. To encourage self-expression.
3. To move students toward divergent, creative thinking.
4. To reward independent thinking.
5. To increase student abilities to question, conceptualize and articulate thoughts.

Elementary Level

The *Elementary Philosophical Inquiry* curriculum utilizes the inquiry method to move students from early concrete mental functioning to early formal reasoning. The inquiry approach:

1. is process oriented and involves simple investigations and problem solving;
2. involves student interactions and cooperative learning skills;
3. utilizes basic thinking skills and thinking skill combinations;
4. is open-ended and flexible, and not based on preconceived teacher expectations;
5. treats students as investigators and requires interpretations and explanations.

Middle /High School Level

The *Middle Grades Philosophical Problem Solving* curriculum, *Cartoons for Thinking*, and the activities in the foundation book *Philosophy for Young Thinkers* employ the following skills:

1. Skill combinations including research, quantitative interpretation, group participation, and social judgment.
2. Problem solving operations involving high concrete and early formal thinking.
3. Formal reasoning processes.

The *PYT* curriculum is a values-centered approach to understanding the major concepts and skills that help define our culture and civilization. Hester and Vincent feel that it is not enough that students learn to think and reason, but that they learn to think and reason in a manner which escapes the biases of past generations, maintaining an objective and morally sensitive view of life. The creation of moral autonomy in students demands that our classrooms become places of discussion and discovery, of openness and freedom of thought.

WHOLE LANGUAGE

The concept of **whole language** grows out of research that shows that students learn language when it is whole, meaningful, and relevant. This philosophy or method of approaching teaching and learning has been articulated by Kenneth Goodman, professor of language and literacy education at the University of Arizona.

He says, (1986) "What we're doing is building written language much the way kids learn oral language, not breaking it up into bits and pieces." The whole language approach is not a specific method of teaching but a set of beliefs, a philosophy. It favors letting teachers and students choose what they read and write about, organizing teaching around "themes," and evaluating children through anecdotal records or "kid watching."

Whole language does not oppose teaching phonics, but opposes teaching any skill or skill set in a fixed sequence. When phonics is taught, it should be integrated into the material being used by teachers and students. Learning and thinking skills are not to be taught in isolation from content materials. If a student is writing a letter to a friend in another school, and the teacher "helps" with this writing (goes through what is called "editing" or "conferencing" with the student), the skills of grammar, reading and thinking will be discussed openly with the student. Although some have claimed that whole language teachers do not teach skills, these teachers claim that they do. They tell us the difference is that they teach skills in context, not in isolation from subject-related and everyday information.

Another name for "whole language" is "integrated language arts," but much more than language arts is being taught here. Through this philosophy, language arts is integrated with science, social studies and mathematics. Learning and thinking skills are also integrated into instruction to complete the integrated curriculum. Whole language teachers encourage budding writers to concentrate first on meaning (conceptual understanding). They also say that the use of "invented spelling" helps children develop an understanding of phonics. It also frees them to experiment with language, concepts, and meanings.

One of the major contributions of whole language instruction is the stimulation of divergent, risk-taking, creative learning. This is significant because it instills in students positive attitudes toward learning as "discovery," as "invention," and as "worthwhile." Whole language is also an affective approach to children that builds and maintains self esteem. Students are not divided into groups from the slowest readers to the fastest readers. Students are not pigeonholed, with the "slower," getting a heavier dose of skills drills.

In the whole language classroom, discovery, inquiry and problem solving are emphasized. Children form and reform groups to work on projects based on shared interest. The artificiality of "cooperative" learning is broken down as children form natural learning groups to work on things of interest to them. They also critique each other's work, offering praise and suggestions. The result is children who love learning, who are able to think and make their own decisions and carry them out.

In 1977, Janet Hickman observed that "fluent readers and writers become fluent by reading and writing a great deal, from things of their own choosing and for their own purpose." Because learning centers can provide opportunities for these kinds of experiences, they play an important role in solidifying a strong foundation for cognitive growth and development as well as for reading/language fluency.

There are major differences between traditional learning centers and developmental language centers. Based on the principle that language develops best in the process of being used (the way all thinking develops), activities in a developmental language center are designed for a child's independent practice level, not for a child's instructional level.

The chart in Figure 7.1 provides a comparative look at the traditional concept of centers and those found in a language development center.

> All children have immense language resources when they enter school. By understanding and respecting and building on the language competence of children we can make literacy an extension of the natural language of children.
>
> —Ken Goodman

FUTURE PROBLEM SOLVING

For the past decade and a half, students from all over the United States and many other countries have been participating in the *Future Problem Solving Program*. This program is built on the problem solving model, adds scenario writing and creative thinking to it, and focuses on some of the complex challenges facing society today. According to Anne

Figure 7.1: Traditional and Developmental Language Centers

Traditional Center	Developmental Language Center
1. Specific tasks	1. Choice of activities
2. Worksheets	2. books, real life materials, concrete manipulatives
3. Time limit	3. No time limits
4. Rotation of groups	4. Child-centered sequence
5. Groups are static	5. Groups are heterogeneous and fluid
6. Instructional-level activites	6. Independent-level practice
7. Teacher directed	7. Teacher modeled, child directed
8. Specific outcome	8. Child selected/produced outcomes
9. External consolidation	9. Internal motivation and consolidation of skills and understandings
10. Task centered	10. Child-centered

Children are placed in specific groups which operate according to clocked rotations. Each child progresses through a predetermined sequence of learning activities, completing specific tasks according to established goals and objectives set up by the teacher.	Children operate with familiar, independent-level materials according to their personal motivations and the length of their interests. Concrete operational-level activities relate to meaningful experiences that children have previously encountered through modeling, guidance or personal endeavors.

Crabbe (1989), these challenges include robotics, acid rain, shrinking tropical forests, energy sources, industrialization of space, genetic engineering, nutrition, poverty, youth and the law, education, the elderly, new forms of employment, immigration, and terrorism. Each year the program focuses on five different topics. These are selected by tens of thousands of students around the world who vote for the topics of greatest interest to them.

> The summer of 1988 saw many regions of the United States parched by drought. Meteorologists speculated that the change in climate was due largely to the Greenhouse Effect, a warming of the earth's atmosphere caused by man-made pollutants. The Greenhouse Effect was a startling new concept to many—but not to students who had studied the topic in the 1984–85 Future Problem Solving Program.
>
> —Anne B. Crabbe

In 1974, E. Paul Torrance, working with a group of high school students in Athens, Georgia, created the *Future Problem Solving Program*. Torrance had two major purposes: (1) to help schools do more to assist students develop their creative talents, and (2) to help students focus on the future that they would encounter as they entered adulthood. Helping students use the creative problem solving process that Alex Osborn (1967) had developed for business and industry, students began to examine problems related to the future. Within ten years, the project had developed into a year long curriculum reaching approximately 175,000 students all over the world.

The Process

The creative problem solving process embodies six major steps:

1. Research and learn as much as possible about a general topic.
2. Brainstorm problems related to the specific situation presented.
3. Identify a major underlying problem from the list of brainstormed problems.
4. Brainstorm solutions to the underlying problem.
5. Develop a list of criteria by which to evaluate the solutions.
6. Evaluate the solutions according to the criteria to select the best solution.

Students, working in teams of four, complete three practice booklets during the year. These booklets contain the results of the team's problem solving efforts. On certain dates, these booklets are sent to trained evaluators to be scored and returned with comments to help the team improve. Finally, the highest-scoring teams receive invitations to participate in State Future Problem Solving Bowls held in the spring. The winning state teams are then invited to participate in the International Future Problem Solving Conference held each June at the University of Michigan.

Practice Problems

Each practice problem begins with a "Fuzzy Situation," a description of a specific situation related to the general topic. The "fuzzies" are futuristic scenarios based on information extrapolated from general knowledge about the topic. After brainstorming problems that might arise in the Fuzzy Situation, the students then turn to identifying a major underlying problem. This problem, when solved, will help solve several other problems. Once agreed upon by the team members, the underlying problem is put into question form, beginning with either "How might we...?" or "In what ways might we...?" When writing their underlying problems, teams will include whatever information they consider relevant.

The lack of a right answer, a fill-in-the-blank approach common in schools today, forces students to make choices. This is the strength of the program. Skill in decision making is practiced and adjusted during the process.

Students must next generate solutions, combining known information with their own creative ideas and thinking of novel ways to solve their problem. Evaluators give extra points for each solution that is unique and still within the realm of possibility. The students complete their booklet by describing their best solution as a proposal for solving the underlying problem.

Program Components

The *Future Problem Solving Program* serves students in all grades, primary through secondary. There is also a component for college students. The Regular Program now serves students in grades 4–12, with divisions based on grade levels. The Primary Division offers a similar format for younger students. The emphasis at the primary level is completely instructional and not competitive.

Another component of the program is the Community Problem Solving Division which challenges students with experience in the program to solve real problems in their own communities. This aspect of the program is growing in popularity and is affecting communities in dramatic ways (Crabbe, 1989).

Skill And Attitude Development

By participating in the *Future Problem Solving Program* students learn about topics that will affect their future. They also learn basic thinking processes crucial to their success in the business world. They learn the process of problem solving and decision making, and the micro-thinking skills supportive of these processes, and they are able to strengthen their communication skills when they find that having a good idea is not enough. They must be able to convey the idea orally and in writing. They learn to analyze and evaluate information directly or indirectly. They quickly learn the difference between fact and opinion as "they become detectives in their pursuit of knowledge" (Crabbe 1989). Torrance (1983) says, "In educating children to think in the future tense and develop vigorous images of the future, we greatly need 'time spanners' to help children swing their thinking to the future. There are no records or witnesses of the future as there are of the past. However, there is human imagination, and scenario writing is one effective vehicle for mobilizing this resource."

THE SCIENTIFIC METHOD

There is in our schools today a great emphasis placed on science and the scientific method. Schools annually hold science fairs and states participate in Science Olympiad programs. It is generally agreed that the pursuit of knowledge is one of our most distinctively human characteristics. Therefore, I presume that it is natural to be concerned with the method by which knowledge is acquired. A question such as "How do you know?" reflects our everyday concern with problems of method.

Most of us would agree that dreams, guesses and hunches are, on the whole, not reliable ways of acquiring dependable beliefs. We would probably be skeptical if someone insisted that strange animals had inhabited the earth at an early period of history, simply because s/he had dreamed that it was so. If, on the other hand, s/he arrived at his or her belief by some acceptable method, we would be much more likely to credit this person's claim. To put the matter differently, it is clear that we do not regard a person as having real knowledge, or even a dependable belief or opinion, unless s/he has acquired the knowledge or belief by some method that we endorse as sound.

The intimate connection between knowledge and method leads to a host of questions. How much can we hope to know? Are there limits beyond which our knowledge can never penetrate? Can we know anything for certain? If so, what can be known for certain, and how do we discover it? If not, what kind of warrant do we have for such beliefs as we hold?

In the history of thought a number of ways for acquiring knowledge have been recommended. Each of these methods makes special claims, emphasizing the extent of its application, or the certainty of its conclusions, or the importance of the questions with which it can deal. These methods range from a reliance on the senses (empirical), to reason (rational), to feelings (intuitional), and to beliefs (authority). Since the method of science seems to be the most reliable and acceptable method for acquiring knowledge in our times, in this section we will outline its component parts.

The Method of Science

Scientific inquiries pursue common aims by a common method. The scientific method has the following characteristics:

1. It is empirical, relying on experience in two different ways: (a) scientists search for data as a basis on which to found beliefs and theories, and (b) scientists seek to confirm or refute theories by a further appeal to experience.
2. All data directly relevant to a problem must be investigated.
3. Hypotheses and theories must be precisely and explicitly formulated.
4. Alternative hypotheses are to be tested with reference to the consequences that follow from them.
5. An attempt must be made—in any field of inquiry—to find a consistent set of hypotheses that take into account as many facts as possible.

6. Scientists stress the repeatability and public verifiability of their observations.
7. Scientists employ mathematical formulations wherever possible (for consistency and reliability, thus joining reason and experience).
8. Scientists use experimental methods to test alternative hypotheses.
9. Scientists desire to extend the range of applicability of any hypothesis to include as much data as they can.

In everyday life we rarely sift or scrutinize the data on which our beliefs are based, and we rarely make further conscious, explicit tests to see if our beliefs are actually confirmed or justified. In science no theory is regarded as acceptable unless these conditions have been satisfied. It is evident that the procedures of science represent a refinement of those of everyday life and a more rigorous application of them.

The Purpose of Science

Science consists neither of observations alone nor of inferences alone; its aim is to formulate general explanatory hypotheses that are based on, and confirmed by, the facts that observations and experiments establish. Thoughtful persons have long realized that the decisive respect in which contemporary societies differ from earlier civilizations is in changes due to mastery and application of science. People alive today are not noticeably more gifted in intelligence, moral insight, or artistic imagination than those of an earlier time. Yet hardly more than 150 years of intense scientific activity have given modern men and women almost godlike powers to remake the very stuff of the universe itself. The invention of the technical weapons used in the 1991 Middle East War by the United States was hardly needed to demonstrate that the understanding and control of science are cardinal conditions for survival of civilizations; and understanding is a necessary preliminary to control.

According to Max Black (1946), the scientific method emphasizes the following purposes:

1. the importance of experience and the use of the senses;
2. the choice of significant, deliberate, intentional and directed observations;

3. the discarding of certain experiences as illusory;
4. public verification and the elimination of bias.

This last point is particularly important and stressed by Irving M. Copi (1953): "The sound experimental criticism of a hypothesis is subordinated to certain moral conditions; in order to estimate correctly the agreement of a physical theory with the facts, it is not enough to be a good mathematician and skillful experimenter; one must also be an impartial and faithful judge."

Although we are unable to deal with the pros and cons of the scientific method in this chapter, as teachers we must be on guard for changes in method, for proven weaknesses, and substantiated strengths. It is a basic principle of scientific inquiry that no proposition is to be accepted without adequate grounds. As teachers, our role is the continual evaluation of these grounds.

THE PAIDEIA PROPOSAL

The *Paideia Program* (1984) completes a trilogy projected by the members of the Paideia Group to expound and explain their proposed reform of basic schooling in the United States. According to Mortimer Adler, founder of the group:

> The main goal of *The Paideia Proposal* as an educational manifesto calling for a radical reform of basic schooling in the United States is to overcome the elitism of our school system from its beginning to the present day, and to replace it with a truly democratic system that aims not only to improve the quality of basic schooling in this country, but also to make that quality accessible to all our children.

Citing John Dewey, Adler notes that all children are destined for leisure, learning and labor. All have the same three elements in their futures: the demands of work, the duties of citizenship, and the obligation of each individual to make the most of h/herself, and to lead rich and fulfilling lives. Adler says that "their treatment in school should be such that it serves these three fundamental purposes for all."

Adler brings to our attention five errors which, in his opinion, need correction:

1. The error of supposing that only some, not all, children are educable and that only some, not all, have a human right to aspire to become truly educated human beings in the course of their lives. We hold the very opposite: that all are educable in exactly the same sense of the term, and that all have the human right to become educated in their mature years.

2. The error of thinking that the process of education takes place and reaches completion in our educational institutions during the years of basic schooling and in advanced schooling after that. Nothing could be further from the truth. No one has ever been and no one can ever become educated in the early years of life. Education happens only with continued learning in adult life.

3. The error of regarding teachers as the sole, primary or principal cause of the learning that occurs in students. The truth here is that the primary cause of learning is the activity of the learner's own mind. Teachers are at best only a secondary cause, an instrumental aid, assisting the process by occasioning and guiding the mental activity of the learners in their charge.

4. The error of assuming that there is only one kind of learning and one kind of teaching, the kind that consists of the teacher's lecturing or telling and the students' learning what they hear said or find in textbook assignments. There are two other kinds of teaching, coaching and discussing, both more important than the first kind because their results are long-lasting, as the results of the first kind are not.

5. The error of maintaining that schooling is preparation for earning a living. Schooling should include that preparation, but it is the least important of the three objectives of basic schooling.

Although the Paideia Program seeks to establish a course of study that is general, liberal, and humanistic, its most distinctive contribution is what Adler calls the **What, Why, and How of It**. That is, what is to be learned, why it is to be learned, and how it is to be learned with the help of teachers.

WHAT-   Knowledge, skills, and understandings

HOW-   Didactic teaching, coaching that forms the habits through which all skills are possessed, and Socratic teaching by questioning and by conducting discussions of the answers

---

Figure 7.2 illustrates the major thrust of the Paideia Program, especially its importance for the teaching of thinking and for understanding.

Figure 7.2: The Paideia Program

Column One	Column Two	Column Three
Acquisition of Organized Knowledge	Development of Intel-Skills and Skills of Learning	Enlarged Understanding of Ideas and Values

— by means of —

Didactic instruction lectures and responses	Coaching, exercises and supervised practices	Maieutic or Socratc questioning and active participation

In three areas of...	**In the operations of...**	**In the...**
Language, literature, the fine arts Mathematics Natural science History, geography social studies	Reading, writing Speaking, listening Calculating Problem solving Observing, measuring Estimating Exercising critical judgement	Discussion of books and works of art and involvement in artistic activities, e. g. music, drama, visual arts

CHAPTER EIGHT

Building a Teaching-for-Thinking School

ॐ

SELLING THE VISION

Objectives

Project: thinking works begins with the following assumptions:

1. Schools should make certain that all students learn to the optimum of their ability.
2. Optimal learning implies the ability to think critically and to utilize reasoning processes which combine critical thinking skills into patterns to increase cognitive productivity.
3. Planned instruction that is developmentally appropriate based on diagnostic information will greatly enhance learning productivity.
4. The goal of teaching-for-thinking is to supply a repertoire of experiences and actions a student requires if s/he is to have the data to reflect upon and the data from which s/he will be able to grow cognitively from concrete to formal thinking ability.
5. Teaching-for-thinking should be blended with the basic components of mastery teaching and mastery learning:

   Learning objectives. Learning objectives will effectively blend thinking skills with the whole school curriculum.

   Instructional practices. Instructional practices should focus on mastery teaching and mastery learning and include knowledge of the programs reviewed in chapter seven of this manual.

   Feedback correctives for remediation and enrichment. Feedback from students to teachers through regular evaluation will provide an information base for developing remediation activities or enrichment activities. Remediation will be designed to re-teach for skill improvement (the **associative stage**) and enrichment activities will be designed to both *strengthen* and *tune* the integration of skills across the curriculum.

The task of teaching-for-thinking can be summarized in the following way:

1. Schools should provide a conceptual base that defines thinking and demonstrates how thinking skills can be integrated across the curriculum.
2. Teachers should state learning objectives that integrate **thinking** with whatever is being taught by specifying content objectives, content-skill objectives and thinking objectives in an integrated format.
3. Teachers should use a diagnostic/prescriptive method to discover when, where and how to introduce appropriate thinking skills into instruction.
4. A variety of instructional practices (those which have been proven effective) should be used allowing for teacher selection, and trial and error.
5. Assessment techniques, such as those provided by Patricia Arlin (1987), should be use to evaluate cognitive ability.
6. Feedback correctives for remediation and enrichment should not only improve learning but teaching as well.
7. Staff development should be provided that allows for the development of thinking among teachers and an understanding of the goals of the project.

Project Planner

Project Description. *Project: Thinking Works* is recommended for development over a period of three years as a plan for infusing teaching-for-thinking into the whole school curriculum. This project will include an overview of thinking, thinking skills, staff development, and requisite materials.

Project Purpose.
1. To restructure teaching practices for teaching-for-thinking.

2. To include teaching-for-thinking in every lesson, every day.
3. To develop an assessment instrument—to be used by teachers—to increase the effectiveness of appropriate classroom instruction.

Project Strategy
1. Develop overall plan, project and staff development guide.
2. Provide thinking skills model and definition of appropriate thinking skills.
3. Include all faculty in planning and assessment.

Personnel Requirement.
1. Training specialist for initial training.
2. Subject area specialists for detail training and follow-up.

Status.
1. Form task force for initial research and development of project.
2. Provide teachers with overall plan, project guide and staff development plan.
3. Develop a calendar of activities and set starting date.

BUILDING A FOUNDATION

Training

The ability to teach-for-thinking requires teachers to become excellent thinkers. This means that they must restructure their own cognitive processes and, hence, the way they teach. Staff development for teaching-for-thinking will be a continuous process, but will be more intense during the first two to three years as teachers develop ways of infusing thinking into already established teaching plans and methodologies.

We must remember that every teacher will be involved in teaching-for-thinking. This includes regular academic teachers and support teachers from the arts, physical education, foreign languages and exceptional children. No matter what cognitive levels we discover among the diversity of students who come into our classes, we must reinforce the critical thinking and academic skills that they have previously mastered and make an effort to move them forward to the next level of cognitive development.

On-going assessment can be carried out by the classroom teacher in a continuous flow of teaching, remediation and enrichment activities. Diagnostic as well as antidotal feedback will support our instructional efforts as we remove artificial barriers to learning—textbook domination, grade leveling, inadequate grouping patterns, etc.—and as we provide developmentally appropriate learning activities that induce cognitive growth and intellectual maturation.

Suggested inservice for teachers. Intensive staff development will occur during the first two to three years of the program. This will include the following:

Year One:
1. Ten hour overview of the project and the critical thinking skills appropriate for each cognitive level (all faculty).
2. One day training for teachers of mathematics, exceptional children and students-at-risk.
3. At least four classroom visitations and conferences with these teachers during the first year by a training specialist.

Year Two:
1. One-half day overview and evaluation workshop for all faculty focusing on instructional problems (strengthening and tuning).
2. One day training for content area teachers (science, social studies, language arts) and other teachers (physical education, art, drama, music, foreign languages, etc.).
3. At least four classroom visitations and conferences with these teachers during the year by training specialist.

Year Three:
1. Ten hour workshop for all teachers.
2. One conference with each teacher (or special group).
3. Program evaluation by selected teacher/administrator task force.

Teaching

Both theory and practice indicate that an effective synthesis of classroom teaching and thinking skills will produce better learning outcomes and respond to a growing pressure to serve all students. In order to help us include teaching-for-thinking into the school curriculum, the *Effective Thinking Skills Model* has been developed which represents a blending of thinking skills with regular subject content, effective schools research, mastery teaching and learning, teaching and learning styles, developmental theory, and creativity.

Thomas R. Guskey (1990) provides the following guidelines for synthesizing these different innovative strategies for improving teaching-for-thinking:

1. All innovative strategies in the improvement program should share common goals and premises.
2. No single innovative strategy can do everything.
3. The innovative strategies in the improvement program should complement each other.
4. All innovative strategies need to be adapted to individual classrooms and building conditions.
5. When a well-conceived combination of innovative strategies is used, the results are likely to be greater than those attained by using any single strategy.

The strategies recommended in the *Effective Thinking Skills Model* include:

Strategy 1:Learning objectives
1. Factual information
2. Concepts and generalizations
3. Distinct human values
4. Skills (subject related and thinking skills)

Strategy 2: Instructional practices
1. Mastery teaching
2. Developmental approaches
3. Coaching
4. Teaching styles
5. Creativity
6. Problem solving

Strategy 3: Feedback correctives
1. Evaluations

2. Mastery learning
3. Learning styles
4. Cooperative learning

Strategy 4: Blending thinking skills and subject matter
1. Evaluation of thinking skills programs and materials
2. Yearly planning for thinking skills infusion
3. Utilization of **lesson plan guide** for thinking skills infusion

Teaching Environment

The teaching environment which encourages thinking and intellectual development will be an enabling environment. Such an environment will develop in every student the capacity to succeed. *The goal is achievement.* The achiever is one who:

1. is able to understand and follow directions;
2. is motivated;
3. has established a pattern of success;
4. has a strong memory function;
5. is able to organize and plan;
6. is able to process information, and;
7. is involved in learning both in and out of school.

Motivating students toward these achievement patterns, towards a desire to learn, requires a learning environment with the following characteristics:

1. It improves the student's ability to use thinking skills, inquiry and problem solving, and verbalize the results of their work.
2. It provides for both individual and group instruction, remediation and enrichment.
3. It teaches the science of thought and develops the art of using one's intelligence.
4. It employs teaching methods in which thinking processes are infused into subject matter.
5. It encourages divergent thinking, the creative use of the imagination, and alternative approaches to solving problems.

6. It helps students transfer skills learned in the classroom to every-day situations and problems.

The teaching environment, especially one that encourages and pro-motes critical thinking and creativity, must be supportive rather than critical, growth producing rather than satisfied with the status quo, and positive rather than defensive. E. Paul Torrance (1963) reminds us of the importance of falling in love with "something." He comments:

> Many people have no dream, no clear image of the future. Some have a dream, even a clear image of the future but they are not in love with it—they may feel that it is not really them. How might one search for her/his identity and discover a dream and fall in love with it? In my opinion, this search for identity is one of the most important things that a person ever does. It has been a basic concern of my re-search.

We now know that self identity and the development of one's intelli-gence cannot be considered separately. They are a part of the same pack-age called "self." It is important, therefore, that teachers teach-for-think-ing and allow students to explore all of their "possible" futures. This requires a learning environment that includes basic thinking skills and the thought processes by which students are able to recognize, under-stand and sort out the possibilities that lie before them.

DEVELOPING A PROGRAM

This section is a checklist of those actions required to develop an ef-fective teaching-for-thinking program. There may be other items that you wish to add to this list. What is presented here are simply those items considered to be basic to any program development.

Program Planning

☐ Planning team selected
☐ Project purposes defined
☐ Project goals written

- [ ] Personnel requirements outlined
- [ ] Status defined regularly:
  - [ ] Program inception
  - [ ] Status at end of first six months
  - [ ] Status at end of first year
  - [ ] Status at middle of second year
  - [ ] Status at end of second year
  - [ ] Status at middle of third year
  - [ ] Status at end of third year
  - [ ] Program needs at end of third year

2. Target Areas

- [ ] Exceptional Children
- [ ] Students-At-Risk
- [ ] Regular Students
- [ ] Gifted Students

EVALUATING THE PROJECT

Needs Assessment for Project: Thinking Works

A needs assessment is a method for identifying discrepancies between what exists and what is needed or intended. A needs assessment serves two major purposes:

1. it establishes the parameters for developing new programs, and
2. it uses staff input as a first step in creating teacher awareness of needs.

The needs analysis is essential for justifying resources that will be requested for the program. The assessment should reflect an examination of evidence supporting the presence of *need, programs now in place that meet these needs, needed changes in existing programs, program philosophy, and fiscal responsibility.*

Figure 8.1: Information Sheet

Date: _____

1. Student name _____

2. Pre-test results:

   skill level _____

   skill target (conquest area) _____

3. Post-test results: _____

4. Skill area focus:

   ☐ Study skills _____

   ☐ Test-taking skills _____

   ☐ Content related skills _____

   ☐ Thinking skills _____

5. Materials needed: _____

   _____

6. Teacher training required to meet needs of student _____

   _____

7. Parent involvement _____

   _____

1.0 Philosophy

1.1 Written philosophy
1.2 Program description (present and future changes)
1.3 Existing resources
1.4 Needed resources
1.5 Involvement of key individuals/groups
   a. Central Office
   b. Principals
   c. Teachers
   d. Parents
   e. Community agencies
1.6 Written plan (functions to justify the program)

2.0 Goals and Objectives

The single most critical component of any program is the statement of goals and objectives. Goals provide the direction for selection and/or creation of measurable objectives. Measurable objectives provide direction for selecting student learning activities and evaluation strategies. A clear statement of goals will insure that the population of students in the program is being served adequately.

2.1 Goals

Goal 1.0
   Objective 1.1
   Objective 1.2
   Objective 1.3

Goal 2.0
   Objective 2.1
   Objective 2.2
   Objective 2.3

Goal 3.0
   Objective 3.1
   Objective 3.2
   Objective 3.3

2.2 Elements. Does each objective contain the four essential elements required to define direction for program development?

Who will demonstrate the changed or new behavior?

How much may be stated as a statistically significant change?

Behavior. What specific behavior will be demonstrated by those changed?

Condition. Under what conditions will the behavior be demonstrated?

2.3 Means. Do you currently have an instrument or means for assessing the behavior defined in each objective?

2.4 Decisions. Does each objective lend itself to clearcut decisions about instructional activities appropriate for students in the program?

3.0 Identification. Identification is a two stage process involving an initial screening of the entire school for evidence of thinking ability and level.

3.1 What assessment instrument has been selected for each level?

3.2 How are results of assessment used by teachers to modify instruction?

3.3 Are evaluations used for remediation and enrichment purposes?

3.4 What classroom patterns/groupings are used (if any) for thinking instruction?

3.5 How are end-of-year evaluation results used for future placement and by teachers in the next grade?

3.6 How have parents been involved? What training has been provided for parents?

4.0 Program of instruction. A program of instruction must reflect the infusion of teaching-for-thinking in the instructional practices of teachers; that is, it must include the goals and objectives of the program.

4.1 Have teachers made yearly plans for thinking skills infusion?

4.2 Has team planning occurred for thinking skills infusion?

4.3 Are curriculum guides being prepared for thinking skills infusion?

4.4 Are any student groupings being prepared according to thinking skills levels?

4.5 Has a material needs assessment been prepared?

5.0 Staff development. Teaching-for-thinking skills infusion will require teacher training.

5.1 What workshops, college courses, etc. have been included in teacher staff development plans?
5.2 What support services are being provided for teachers?
5.3 What follow-up staff development plans have been arranged?
5.4 What procedures for maintaining student assessment records have been provided?

6.0 Funding. What provisions have been made for the consistent funding of the project?

6.1 Has a budget been prepared for each school? for the school district?
6.2 Does the budget require additional funds (more than normally provided)? If so, how are these funds to be obtained?
6.3 How can the program be modified to become cost effective?

7.0 Community awareness-parent involvement. Briefly describe measures to involve the community and parents in the development, growth, and continuance of the project.

8.0 Program evaluation
8.1 What annual program evaluation measures have been established?
8.2 What evaluation measures have been established to ensure internal program consistency?
8.3 Is there a three-year or a five-year plan in place for program development?

THINKING SKILLS SUMMARY
K–3 Thinking Skills

Perceptual Skills:

K-Observing, collecting, describing
1-Comparing, characterizing by resemblance

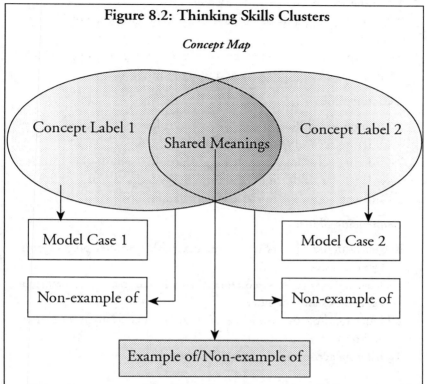

Figure 8.2: Thinking Skills Clusters

Concept Map

Concept Label 1

Shared Meanings

Concept Label 2

Model Case 1

Model Case 2

Non-example of

Non-example of

Example of/Non-example of

Concepts are a set of attributes common to any and all instances of a given class, type, kind or category.

Concept example is any and all indivdual items that have the characteristics of a given concept.

Concept nonexample is any and all individual items that may have some but not all the characteristics of a given concept.

A **model case** is an example of a concept which one feels completely sure is an instance of the concept.

2-Exploring, finding new relationships
3-Looking for interrelationships

Classifying Skills:

K-Listing and matching according to known categories

1-Sorting by similarities and differences

2-Understanding and using concepts—belonging to, not belonging to

3-Creating new groupings by combining smaller groups which share a common property and using multiple attributes

Seriating Skills

K-Ordering according to size, shape and color

1-Ordering according to volume, pitch and tempo

2-Ordering according to increasing/decreasing sound, pitch, shade, color, from left to right; and from heavy to its reverse.

3-Ordering according to cause-effect relationships

Sequencing Skills:

K-Reproducing objects in a sequence with a model present and from memory

1-Ordering events in a sequence through actions, words, written expressions and memory

2-Understanding the sequence of natural events, language, stories and time

3-Ordering according to cause/effect events

Questioning Skills

Questioning directly related to Problem Solving Model:

1. What makes a decision necessary?
   What are the facts?
   What/Who is responsible for the problem?
2. What are my options?
   What could I do?
   Which options are best?
3. What the consequences?
   What is the value of the consequences?
4. How can I do it?
   What is the best option?
   How do I know which option is best?

Question types based on the "Management of Information" model:

1. Gathering Questions: Who? When? What? Why? Where? How?
2. Organizing questions: Why?
3. Extending questions: What next...? What if...?

Stages of Skill Acquisition (see page 78):

1. *The interpretive stage.* Taught by declarative representations, verbal directives, and verbal characterizations.
   Students verbally rehearse the information required to execute the skill using new knowledge and experience to provide meaning.
2. *The associative stage.* The associative stage functions to smooth out the skill. Here the student will detect and eliminate errors.
   Students will discover why (causal explanation) and will clarify significant concepts.
3. *The autonomous stage.* Strengthening and tuning processes are used to integrate and improve the skill. Should be able to independently use the skill.

The Inquiry Method

Major inquiry Processes:

1. Describing
2. Explaining
3. Predicting
4. Choosing

Steps of Inquiry Implementation:

1. State the problem to be solved clearly and simply.
2. Discuss the problem-situation and then construct a tentative answer to it called a "hypothesis."
3. Investigate the problem (test and evaluate the hypothesis).
4. Formulate a solution to the problem.
5. Review the whole process/get feedback from a friend.
6. Write solution and present it to the class.

Figure 8.3: Skill Clusters Related to Inquiry

ATTRIBUTING

Purpose: To describe the characteristics of people, places, things, events, ideas, etc.

Related Skills:
Comparing/contrasting
Classifying
Sequencing
Seriating

Major skill extension:

Comparing and Contrasting

Clarifying ideas
Significant similarities and differences
Significant patterns and concepts
Interpreting significant similarities and differences

INFERRING

Purpose: Making statements about the unknown on the basis of the known.

Related Skills:
Hypothesizing
Predicting
Generalizing (drawing conclusions)
Analyzing relevant/irrelevant data

Major skill extension:

Analyzing

Analyzing for bias
Evaluating assumptions
Checking for consistency
Searching for casual explanation

CAUSAL EXPLANATION

Purpose: Assessing how well new data fits what else we know.

Related Skills:
Searching for causes
Accounting for or against the likelihood of a conclusion
Assessing relevant evidence
Explaining relationships

Major skill extension:

Explaining

Connecting bits and pieces of information
Gaining overall picture of how things work
Ranking rival conclusions in order of plausibility
Judging relevance of new information

EVALUATING

Purpose: Expressing approval or disapproval for alternative solutions.

Related skills:
Prioritizing
Assessing reliability of evidence
Establishing criteria of valuation
Generalizing
Making decisions

Major skill extension:

Generalizing

Formulating simple hypotheses
Statement of observation reports
Testing observation reports to determine if they confirm or falsify the generalization

Figure 8.4 Problem Solving Steps and Strategies

Step One: The Analysis of Problems	Strategy Focus

A. Recognizing a problem exists
B. Identifying a problem
    of identification
    of causation
    of means
    of ends
C. Stating the problem clearly
D. Stating the problem usefully
	1. The anaylsis of problems
	2. Comparing ideas, concepts
	3. Describing facts, events, problems

Step Two: The Formation of Hypotheses	**Strategy Focus**
A. Collecting information B. Making information management C. Writing the hypothesis D. Writing the proto-hypotheses should come at the beginning of the investigation	1. Comparing Information 2. Evaluating solutions 3. Explaining causal relationships
Step Three: Examining and Testing the Hypotheses	**Strategy Focus**
A. Recognizing assumptions B. Developing implications C. Examining implications D. Interpreting observations E. Drawing conclusions	1. Evaluating solution alternatives 2. Comparing conclusions/answers 3. Explaining Causal relationships

Glossary

❧

Attribute cluster. Groups of thinking skills that are similar in purpose and in function.

Concept. Mental/abstract category of a fact.

Creativity. A modality of thinking including originality, flexibility, risk-taking and incubation.

Cognitive development. The growth in intellectual ability including the ability to use thinking skills and processes in cognitive development.

Concrete operations. Thinking operations that allow students to apply their thinking to concrete objects and situations but not to abstract/formal ideas and processes.

Cognitive restructuring. Revising old thinking methods, acquiring new ways of thinking, and intelligent processes to combat and relieve ignorance.

Data-driven thinking. Inductive, and relatively automatic, thinking that is open to the environment and is flexible and experience-dependent.

Developmental approaches. Developmental refers to bringing instruction and materials into a consistent relationship with students' social and cognitive ability.

Encapsulated thinking. Thinking that is limited by cultural biases.

Epistemic correlations. An agreement reached through two or more valid approaches to knowledge.

Facilitating skills. Micro-thinking processes necessary for performing all other thinking opertions.

Fact. A fact is "that which is…"

Feedback correctives. Information received through student assessment essential to remediation and enrichment activities.

Formal operational skills. Eight concepts identified as highly complex and abstract which employ facilitating and processing skills in their development.

Goal-driven thinking. Thinking that responds to internal signals, is consciously learned, and works in a step-by-step fashion.

Inferences. Statements about the unknown made on the bias on the known.

Inquiry. A method of diagnosis, speculation and hypothesis testing that—in this manual—is a concrete thinking procedure leading to formal problem solving.

Judgments. Statements that express approval or disapproval of occurrences, persons, objects or alternative solutions to a problem.

Learning objectives. The association of thinking skills and subject content in a developmentally appropriate manner for the purpose of focusing and narrowing instruction.

Learningful organization. An organization characterized by systems thinking, personal mastery, mental models, a shared vision and team learning.

Mastery teaching. A method which assumes that all students can learn and that teachers must respond to student needs. This method utilizes frequent assessment and feedback correctives.

Operational skills. Skills characterized by the ability of students to think abstractly and propositionally, including the ability to use formal reasoning and formal problem solving procedures.

Organizing skills. Facilitating skills of classifying, sequencing and seriating.

Perceptual skills. Facilitating skills based on (experiencing) sensing spatial relationships.

Problem-solving. A continual movement back and forth from thought to word and from word to thought. Every thought tends to connect something with something else, establishing a relationship between things. Every thought moves, grows and develops, fulfills a function, and solves a problem (Johnson-Laird).

Processing skills. Skills that enable students to process ideas simultaneously and group them according to multiple attributes.

Production. Inquiry or procedural learning.

Proto-hypothesis. An assumed proposition that helps us collect and organize information but which will probably be modified due to research and analysis.

Questioning skills. The beginning of the problem solving, critical thinking process.

Restructuring for critical thinking (RCT). Our capacity to reconstruct our thinking in ways that make learning and teaching more responsive and efficient.

Report words. Declarative statements that describe what one has experienced.

Stages of skill acquisition. A three-step procedure of learning basic or critical thinking skills.

Thinking. A name for a course of action insofar as it is intelligently directed, that is to say, as aims ends enter into it, with selection of means to further the attainment of ends (see Dewey on "mind").

Thinking aloud. A meta-cognitive technique of telling another person or group of persons the procedures used in a problem solving exercise as one moves from identifying the problem to its resolution.

Thinking in transition. Thinking that is moving from concrete to formal operations and shares in both, but inconsistently in formal operations, and is characteristic of middle school students.

Thinking skills. Thinking skills include the basic mental operations of perception and recognition, the organization of thought, the storage, retrieval and transformation of data, and deductive/inductive inference.

Thinking skill infusion. Integrating thinking skills into teaching and into subject content on a regular and consistent basis.

Values. Beliefs and assumptions about facts and concepts.

Bibliography

⌘

Adler, Mortimer J. *The Paideia Program*. New York: Macmillan Publishing Company, 1984.

Armstrong, David. Evaluation: Conscience of the social studies. The Social Studies. 1977.

Anderson, John. *The Architecture of Cognition*. Cambridge, MA: Harvard University Press, 1983.

Argyris, Chris. *Overcoming Organizational Defenses*. New York: Prentice-Hall, 1990.

Arlin, Patricia K. *Teaching for Thinking: The Arlin Test of Formal Reasoning Applied*. East Aurora, NY: Slosson Educational Publications, 1987.

Arredondo, D. E. and James H. Block. Recognizing the connections between thinking skills and mastery learning. *Educational Leadership*, 47, (5): 1990.

ASCD, Thinking skills, achievement ranked high in ASCD planning survey, *ASCD Update*. 1983.

Askov, E. N. and K. Kamm. *Study Skills in the Content Areas*. Boston: Allyn and Bacon, 1982.

Ausubel, D. P. and P. Ausubel. Cognitive development in adolescence. *American Education Research Journal*, 1966.

Azbell, Wayne. Supervising the inquiry process. *The Social Studies*. 1977.

Beane, James A. *A Middle School Curriculum, from Rhetoric to Reality*. Columbus, OH: The National Middle School Association, 1990.

Benderson, Robert. Critical thinking: Critical issues. *In Focus 24*. Benderson, Robert (ed.). Princeton, NJ: Educational Testing Service, 1990.

Beyer, Barry K. Conducting moral discussions in the classroom. *Social Education*. 194–202, 1976.

Beyer, Barry K. Improving thinking skills—defining the problem. *Phi Delta Kappan.* 1984.

————. *Practical Strategies for the Teaching of Thinking.* Boston: Allyn and Bacon, 1987.

Black, Howard and Sandy Black. *Organizing Thinking Book II.* Pacific Grove, CA: Midwest Publications, 1990.

Black, Max. *Critical Thinking.* Englewood Cliffs: Prentice-Hall, 1946.

Block, J. H. et al. *Creating Effective Mastery Learning Schools.* New York: Longman, 1989.

Bloom, B. S. Learning for mastery. *Evaluation Comment.* 1, 1: 1968.

Bloom, B. S. Helping all children learn in elementary school and beyond. *Principal.* 67, 4: 1988.

Bloom, B. S. and Lois Broder. *Problem Solving Presses of College Students.* Chicago: University of Chicago Press, 1950.

Brandt, R. S. On research and school organization: A conversation with Bob Slavin. *Educational Leardership.* 46, 2: 1988.

Bransford, J. D. et al. *Anchored Instruction: Why We Need It and How Technology Can Help.* Nashville, TN: Learning Technology Center, George Peabody College, Vanderbilt University, 1988.

Bruner, J. S. *Toward A Theory of Instruction.* New York: Norton, 1966.

Burtt, E. A. *The Search For Philosophic Understanding.* New York: New American Library, 1965.

Butler, Kathleen A. *Learning and Teaching Style.* Columbia, CT: The Learner's Dimension, 1986.

Camp, Bonnie and Mary Bash. *Think Aloud.* Champaign, IL: Research Press, 1981.

Casey, Marion. History as inquiry: Introducing gifted students to history. *The Social Studies.* 1979.

Chomsky, Norm. Review of verbal learning (by B.F. Skinner). *Language.* 35: 1959.

Clark, Barbara. *Growing Up Gifted.* Columbus, OH: Charles E. Merrill, 1979.

Collingwood, Arthur W. *An Essay on Philosophical Method.* Oxford: Clarendon Press, 1933.

Combs, Arthur W. What the future demands of education. *Phi Delta Kappan.* 1981.

Copi, Irving M. *Introduction to logic.* New York: Macmillian, 1953.

Crabbe, Anne B. The future of problem solving. *Educational Leadership.* 47 (1): 1989.

Dewey, John. *How We Think.* Boston: D.C. Heath, 1910.

———. *Democracy and Education.* New York: Macmillan, 1916.

———. *The Quest For Certainty.* New York: Putnam's Sons, 1929.

Dubos, Rene. *The Torch of Life.* New York: Simon and Schuster, Inc., 1962.

Ellis, Arthur and Janet Alleman-Brooks. How to evaluate problem-solving-oriented social studies. *The Social Studies.* 1977.

Ellwood, E. A. *Methods in Sociology.* Durham, NC: Duke University Press, 1933.

Fleischman, Sid. *The Whipping Boy.* Mahwah, NJ: Troll Associates, 1986.

Fogarty, Robin and James Ballanca. *Catch Them Thinking: A Handbook of Classroom Strategies (4–12).* Champaign, IL: Illinois Renewal Institute, 1989.

Frankel, Jack R. *Helping Students Think and Value.* Englewood Cliffs: Prentice-Hall, 1973.

George, Paul. The middle school century. *1988 Journal of the North Carolina League of Middle Level Schools, 10th Anniversary Issue.* 10 (1): 1988.

Glasser, Robert. Variables in discovery learning. In *Learning By Doing, A Critical Approach.* Lee S. Schulman and Evan R. Keoslar (eds.). Chicago: Rand-McNally, 1966.

Goodman, Kenneth. *What's Whole in Whole Language?* Portsmouth, NH: Heinemann Educational Books, 1986.

Gregorc, A. Learning/teaching styles: Potent forces behind them (editorial statement). *Educational Leadership,* 1979.

———. *An Adult's Guide to Style.* Maynard, MA: Gabriel Systems, 1982.

Guskey, Thomas R. *Implementing Mastery Learning.* Belmont, CA: Wadsworth, 1985.

———. Staff development and the process of teacher change. *Educational Researcher.* 15, (5): 1986.

———. Mastery learning and mastery teaching: How they complement each other. *Principal.* 68, (1): 1988.

————. Integrating innovations. *Educational Leadership.* 47, (5): 1990.

Hartoonian, H.M. The first 'R' reasoning. *The Social Studies.* 71, (4): 1980.

Hayakawa, S. I. *Language in Thought and Action.* New York: Harcourt, Brace, 1949.

Herrmann, Ned. *The Creative Brain.* Lake Lure, NC: Brain Dominance Institute, 1987.

Hester, Joe and Philip Vincent. *Philosophy For Young Thinkers.* Monroe, NY: Trillium Press, 1983.

Hester, Joe et al. *Cartoons for Thinking.* Monroe, NY: Trillium Press, 1984.

Hetherington, E. M. and C. W. McIntyre. Developmental psychology. *Annual Review of Psychology.*26: 1975.

Hickman, Janet. What do fluent readers do? *Theory Into Practice.* 1977.

Himsl, Ralph and Garnet Millar. *User's Guidebook, Measure of Questioning Skills.* Athens: The University of Georgia, 1989.

Hunt, Morton. *The Universe Within.* New York: Simon and Schuster, 1982.

Hunter, M. C. Teaching is decision making. *Educational Leadership.* 37, (1): 1979.

————. *Mastery Teaching.* El Segundo, CA: TIP Publications, 1982.

Inhelder, B. and J. Piaget. *The Growth of Logical Thinking from Childhood to Adolescence.* New York: Basic Books, 1964.

Johnson, D. W. and R. T. Johnson. *Learning Together and Alone.* Englewood Cliffs, NJ: Prentice-Hall, 1987.

Johnson-Laird, Philip. *Mental Models.* Cambridge, MA: Harvard University Press, 1983.

Keirsey, David and M. Bates. *Please Understand Me: Character and Temperament Types.* Del Mar, CA: Gnoslogy Books, 1984.

Kerman, S. Teacher expectations and student achievement. *Phi Delta Kappan.* 60: 1979.

Klein, G. S. The personal world through perception. In *Perception: An Approach to Personality.* R. Blake and G. Ramsey (eds.), New York: Ronald Press, 1951.

Kohlberg, L. and R. Mayer. Development as the aim of education. *Harvard Educational Review.* 6: 1972.

Langford, Peter. *Children's Thinking and Learning in the Elementary School.* Lancaster, PA: Technomic Publishing, 1989.

Larkin, J. H. et al. Models of competence in solving physics problems. *Cognitive Science.* 4: 1980.

Lindsay, P. H. and D. A. Norman. *Human Information Processing: An Introduction to Psychology.* New York: Academic Press, 1977.

Lowell, W. E. The development of hierarchical classification skills in science. *Journal of Research in Science Teaching.* 17 (33): 1980.

———. An empirical study of a model of abstract learning. *Science Education.* 61 (42): 1977.

———. A study of hierarchical classification in concrete and abstract thought. *Journal of Research in Science Teaching.* 16 (62): 1979.

Lowery, L. *Thinking and Learning.* Pacific Grove, CA: Midwest Publications, 1989.

Marzano, R. J., et al. *Dimensions of Thinking: A Framework for Curriculum and Instruction.* Alexandria, VA: ASCD, 1988.

Marzano, R. J. and D. E. Arredondo. *Tactics For Thinking.* Alexandria, VA: ASCD, 1986.

Marzano, R. J. et al. Integrating instructional programs through dimensions of learning. *Educational Leadership.* 47 (5): 1990.

Meek, Margaret. *Learning to Read.* London: Bodley Head, 1982.

Miller, G. W. *Questioning Skills Handbook.* Athens: The University of Georgia, 1990.

Milner, E. *Human Neural and Behavioral Development.* Springfield, IL: Charles C. Thomas, 1967.

Mishra, S. P. Cognitive growth in adolescence. In *Contemporary Adolescence: Readings.* H. D. Thornburg (ed.) Monterey, CA: Brooks Cole, 1975.

National Commission on Excellence in Education. *A Nation At Risk.* Washington, DC: U. S. Government Printing Office, 1983.

Neisser, U. *Cognitive Psychology.* New York: Appleton, 1967.

Newell, A. and H. A. Simon. *Human Problem-Solving.* Englewood Cliffs, NJ: Prentice-Hall, 1972.

Nickerson, R. S. et al. *The Teaching of Thinking.* Hillsdale, NJ: Lawrence Erlbaum Associates, 1985.

Northrop, F. S. C. *The Logic of the Sciences and the Humanities.* New York: Macmillan, 1947.

Osborn, A. F. *Applied Imagination.* New York: Charles Scribner's, 1967.

Paul, Richard. *Critical Thinking Handbook: 6th–9th Grades.* Rohnert Park, CA: Sonoma State University, 1989.

Pascale, Richard and A. Athos. *The Art of Japanese Management.* New York: Simon and Schuster, 1981.

Piaget, J. *The Language and Thought of the Child.* London: Routledge, 1926.

————. *Understanding Causality.* New York: Norton, 1974. (*Les Explications Causales.* Paris: Presses Universitaries de France, 1971).

————. *Success and Understanding.* Cambridge, MA: Harvard University Press, 1978.

Piaget, J. and B. Inhelder. *The Psychology of the Child.* New York: Basic Books, 1969.

Piaget, J. *The Construction of Reality of the Child.* New York: Basic Books, 1954.

Posner, M. I. *Chronometric Explorations of Mind.* Hillsdale, NJ: Erlbaum Associates, 1978.

Posner, M. I. and C. R. R. Snyder. Attention and cognitive control. In *Information Processing and Cognition.* R. L. Solso (ed.). Hillsdale, NJ: Erlbaum Associates.

Presseisen, B. Z. *Thinking Skills Throughout the Curriculum.* Bloomington, IN: Pi Lambda Theta, 1987.

Rauhauser, Bill. *Design for Implementing Effective Schools Research.* Lewisville, TX: School Improvement Specialist, 1988.

Rappaport, M. M. and H. Rappaport. The other half of the expectancy equation: Pygmalion. *Journal of Educational Psychology.* 67: 1975.

Report on Education Research. Students lack analytical skills, NAEP says. Denver, CO: National Assessment of Educational Progress, 1981.

Senge, Peter M. *The Fifth Discipline.* New York: Doubleday, 1990.

Slavin, R. E. *Cooperative Learning.* White Plains, NY: Longman, 1983.

Smith, Frank. *Insult to Intelligence.* Portsmouth, NH: Heinemann, 1986.

Smith, Frank (ed.). *Awakening to Literacy.* 1984.

Soled, S. W. Group instructional methods which are as effective as one-to-one tutoring in the improvement of both higher as well as lower mental process achievement. PhD Diss., University of Chicago, 1986.

Spady, W. J. Organizing for results: The basis for authentic restructuring and reform. *Educational Leadership.* 46 (2): 1988.

Sternberg, R. J. How can we teach intelligence? *Educational Leadership.* 42, (1): 1984.

————. Developmental patterns in the encoding and combination of logical connectives. *Journal of Experimental Child Psychology.* 28: 1979.

Suchman, J. Richard. *Developing Inquiry.* Chicago: Science Research Associates, 1975.

Swartz, Bob. Workshop on *Thinking Skills Infusion.* High Point, NC: 1990.

Thornburg, Hershel. Is early adolescence really a stage of development? *1988 Journal of the North Carolina League of Middle Level Schools, 10th Anniversary Issue.* 10 (1): 1988.

Thorndike, E. L. *The Fundamentals of Learning.* New York: Teachers College, 1932.

————. *The Psychology of Wants, Interests, and Attitudes.* New York: Appleton-Century-Crofts, 1935.

Tobias, Shelia. *Overcoming Math Anxiety.* New York: Houghton Miffin, 1980.

Toepfer, Conrad F. Planning gifted/talented middle level school programs: issues and guidelines. *National Association of Secondary School Principals.* 1989.

Torrance, E. Paul. Future problem solving program. In *Teaching Scenario Writing* (revised edition). Cedar Rapids, Iowa: Coe College, 1983.

————. *Education and the Creative Potential.* Minneapolis: University of Minnesota Press, 1963.

Torrance, E. Paul and R. E. Myers. *Creative Learning and Teaching.* New York: Dodd, Mead, 1971.

Torrance, E. Paul. *Learning Styles Handbook.* Athens: University of Georgia, 1977.

Torrance, E. Paul and T. Safter. *The Incubation Model of Teaching.* Buffalo, NY: Bearly Limited, 1990.

Torrance, E. Paul. The importance of falling in love with something. *The Creative Child and Adult Quarterly.* 7 (2): 1983.

Walton, S. and T. Toch. Competency tests linked to decline in analytical skills. *Education Week.* 1 (8): 82.

Whimby, A. and Jack Lochhead. *Problem Solving and Comprehension.* Philadelphia, PA: Franklin Institute Press, 1982.

White, S. H. Evidence for a hierarchical arrangement of learning processes. In *Advances in Child Development and Behavior (Vol. 2).* L. O. Lipaitt and C. C. Spiku (eds). New York: Academic Press, 1965.

Whitehead, A. N. *Adventures of Ideas.* New York: Macmillan, 1933.

Whiteley, J. Control of children's observing responses during information feedback during discrimination learning. *Journal of Experimental Child Psychology.* 39: 1985.

Wilson, John. *Thinking With Concepts.* London: Cambridge University Press, 1963.

Index